eBay Tools & Services Guide 2011

Chris Dawson and Sue Bailey

Published by The Thought Leader Press

Table of Contents

Introduction

TameBay is owned and written by Chris Dawson and Sue Bailey, two British ecommerce professionals. Between us we have traded on eBay for over two decades, and have more than 70,000 positive feedback comments (and just 2 negs!).

Chris and Sue met on eBay UK's PowerSeller forum longer ago than either of them like to admit. By October 2006, both had become frustrated with eBay's inability to keep their users informed of new features on the site, with the impenetrability of eBay's help pages, and with the lack of a UK- and Europe-centered news site for all things ecommercial. In a moment between classes at eBay University, Dan Wilson said what were to be fatal words: *"you need a blog"*. TameBay is the result.

Since the launch in 2006 TameBay has grown to be one of the definitive sources for eBay news, tips, tricks and trading advice. Over 50,000 readers visit the site each month making TameBay one of the best places on the Internet to keep up to date with everything eBay and to network with fellow eBay professional sellers.

We're thrilled to publish the first edition of the TameBay eBay Tools and Services Guide 2011 which brings together all of the tools we've used to run our businesses over the years.

As an eBay business grows there becomes a need to simplify and automate many of the day to day tasks you will be undertaking. Everything from listing an item on eBay, printing and posting your sales, managing your customer communications and expanding your eBay business onto other marketplaces, your own website, shopping comparison sites and using paid search can be done manually. However the use of appropriate tools to manage these processes can automate the functions, perform tasks more effectively and save time and costs freeing you up to manage your business.

Many of the tools in this guide are little known apps which can make a huge contribution to the way you run your eBay business. Others are better known, but you may not have had time to fully investigate the products and services they offer. Whether it is a utility to make printing your labels and invoices automatic, or a fully fledged multi-channel ecommerce management platform you'll find what you're looking for in the following pages.

We'd like to thank all of the companies who have supported us in creating this guide, the many people who support us with content for the site, Dan Wilson for the original suggestion that we should launch TameBay and most importantly of all, you and all our many other thousands of readers who visit TameBay, comment on TameBay and who have made the site what it is today.

For the very latest eBay and ecommerce news don't forget to visit us at TameBay.com.

Best wishes
Sue and Chris

247 TopSeller

247 Top Seller offer a bespoke solution that is cost effective, high quality and efficient for multi-channel ecommerce. Our services include:

- Sell into multiple channels such as eBay (eBay Certified), Amazon, Play.com, Pixmania, Priceminister, your own website and more from one inventory
- Fully Managed Ecommerce technology, design, strategy, account management,customer service and reporting
- Design Services - eBay shop, eBay template, eBay About Me, Amazon WebStore, Facebook
- Full design and integration of Amazon WebStore with multichannel solution (if required)
- Integration of Fulfilment by Amazon for Multichannel order fulfilment by Amazon
- Search Engine Optimisation
- Paid Search
- Feeds Management
- Google, comparison shopping sites, affiliate feeds, specialist feeds
- Comprehensive reporting
- Integration with third-party fulfilment, shipping and accounting partners
- Social Networking
- Consultation and advice
- Integration with Sage 50 and Tradebox
- Full integration with multiple couriers like Royal Mail, Parcel Force, FedEx, DHL, Business
- Post, Home Delivery Network, DPD and more.

Our solution allows you to sell efficiently into multiple channels which will save you valuable time on everyday operations, increase your ROI and cut your overheads.

We operate with integrity and honesty and have a passion for exceeding customer expectations, working to achieve unbeatable standards of quality, productivity and innovation. We pride ourselves on the quality of our Support both in the initial set-up phase and ongoing and will work with you to grow your business to ensure our partnership is a success.

Our HQ is in London and we also have a fully-owned development centre based in India with dedicated staff experienced in application development, design services, managed services and search engine optimisation.

247 TopSeller have developed a great relationship with Amazon, eBay and all the major marketplaces and work closely with them to bring you the solution you need to operate successfully. Our developers are constantly updating the solution with new functionality and we work very hard to keep ahead of the game, which is essential in a fast-moving market.

You can take the complete multi-channel solution or just the parts you require. The Amazon WebStore is offered as a standalone website or as part of the full multi-channel ecommerce solution.

Amazon Webstore

247 TopSeller have worked closely with Amazon to integrate the WebStore into our solution. The WebStore is an ecommerce platform hosted by Amazon and powered by the same technology as Amazon.co.uk, Marks and Spencer, Mothercare and and other major retailers. The WebStore allows you to run your online business in a secure, reliable and scalable environment with minimal financial investment.

Below are some key features of the Amazon WebStore:

- Quick, simple and cost effective.
- Proven track record - uses the same platform as Amazon.co.uk and other major retailers.
- Secure, reliable and scalable.
- Card payments processed by Amazon using the same checkout as their own customers.
- 105 million+ customers can buy without a new account and can use card details already stored with Amazon.
- Highly powerful drag and drop widgets like Best Sellers, Customers Who Also Bought and many other cross and upsell widgets.
- We have a dedicated inhouse WebStore Design and Integration Team who will work with you on a consultative basis.

Amazon Seller Central and Marketplace

Below are some key features of our Amazon solution:

- Allows multiple Marketplace and/or Seller Central accounts for same and/or different countries.
- Full control over shipping price for auto-pricing calculation with competitors.
- Option to exclude specified sellers to avoid competition with trade partners.
- Option to compete with all sellers or those above a certain

seller rank assigned by Amazon.

- Manage all types of item condition eg new, used, collectible, refurbished etc with their sub- conditions.
- Assign default item condition notes to all items based on item condition.
- Restrict the inventory from listing by defining minimum threshold quantity.
- Unlimited access of Amazon database with no restriction of call limits per hour.
- Manage Amazon inventory for all accounts in a single dashboard.
- Synchronise active live listings on Amazon to dashboard.
- Update item details like Item name, Category, Sales Rank, Prices and more direct from Amazon database.
- Easily create new existing item on Amazon for different categories including items with variations like size and colour.
- Change quantity on all channels using a single feed.
- Search various options instantly with live or cached data using Exact, Like or Contains feature.

eBay Marketplace

Below are some key features of our eBay solution:

- Create multiple eBay accounts with different details within the solution.
- Provision for setting shipping, payment, listing design template, listing type, listing days, item specific details, items location etc by account. No need to define these details at item level. Pre-configured item settings to make data entry easier.
- Synchronise active live listings on eBay to the dashboard. No need to end listings when you start using the application.
- Option to change item details in bulk to edit large amounts of inventory in Excel. Can be done using Web-Service integration as well.
- Change quantities on dashboard with live effect.
- Export Selected/Export All Items directly from inventory dashboard.
- Assign shipping and payment profile to a number of items at once.
- Easily manage your item variations by assigning parent child relationship.
- Schedule items for auto listing which can be defined by the seller.
- Monitors and manage all your messages, disputes and and feed backs from the application itself.

We have launched professional eBay store design from £12 per month. User can apply the store design from many options to their stores in matter of minutes. We are also about to launch a listing tool, so that listings have a matching template design. The listing tool combined with the store design will cost from only £25 per month.

Contact us for a no obligation expert consultation.
Our Contact details: Phone: 08000 474 247
Email: request@247topseller.co.uk

Helping small and medium businesses to trade internationally
The ever changing world of technology: whether you see it as a positive or it terrifies you, there is no denying it opens up a world of new opportunities for businesses.

As an online trader, you are now able to find and make contact with companies that you would never have had the opportunity to work with even a mere five years ago. And no company is too small to take advantage of the global market - everyone can benefit from finding lower priced, better quality products and services, or by selling to an increased customer base.

Maggie Choo, Director of International Business Development and Marketing for Alibaba.com globally, comments: *"When it comes to a business experimenting with international trade for the first time, it's easy to overestimate the potential difficulties and underestimate the potential pay back. Thanks to the internet, sourcing opportunities have never been more abundant or varied, allowing small and medium-sized businesses to find all kinds of goods and supplies that they may struggle to source offline. By using online trading platforms and internet searches, they can quickly and easily find off the shelf or bespoke items at a far lower cost.*

Similarly, if you're looking to export, there is a whole world of buyers out there who could be just a couple of clicks away from finding you."

Alibaba.com has compiled the following top tips and insight for companies considering international trade for the first time.

Getting started

- A simple internet search will often bring up a wealth of information. If you're looking for a Chinese manufacturer to help you produce a widget, then type in your search terms and see what happens. Online trading platforms, such as Alibaba.com, can also help to put you in touch with millions of businesses world wide who are ready to trade in that specific category.

Communication

- When communicating with people whose first language is not that of your own, no matter how word-perfect they seem to be, do not over-estimate their language skills.

- Mistakes can sometimes be made so double confirm all the details. Use simple sentence structures, avoid using jargon, acronyms and slang words and make sure you are specific, clear and concise.
- With time differences, communicating has to be well planned and bear in mind this may add extra time to negotiations. Consider local holidays too, when organisations may be closed for an extended period.
- Utilise modern technology to speed the process up. For example, if you're waiting for a product sample from a potential new supplier, ask them to send you a video of it before it is shipped. There may be glaring problems which need addressing, which can then be sorted without waiting for the product to go through transit. Or if you're trying to explain some changes you would like to be made, consider using animation, diagrams or video to explain exactly what you mean.

Embracing differences

- Many people worry about the cultural issues involved when working with a company based in a different country. It's always wise to be sensitive to cultural differences, but don't let those differences put you off getting in touch.
- Avoid making judgments or assumptions about people based on where they are from instead, do a bit of research on Chinese business values, for example, if you plan on dealing with companies in the Far East.
- You may have your mind set on finding the lowest possible price, but don't forget that it is equally (if not more) important to build the relationship as it is to make the deal. Remember you (presumably) are not just in this for a quick fix. You want to find a business partner you can depend on to help your business grow.
- Check if the supplier is already working with businesses in your country for references and to gauge their understanding of your culture. For example, if you're looking at producing clothing, companies in the Far East may not always be geared up to deal with European sizes. Their idea of XL may be very different to yours.

Finances

- Get specialist advice on the financial aspects/tax implications of importing and exporting and make sure this is factored into the price you can afford to pay/charge.

- Be sure to clearly agree payment terms before any transaction takes place. In you are purchasing, be cautious of businesses that ask for cash payment, as that can be a favourite with scammers because a cash transfer is not protected and it's basically like handing cash over to a stranger on the street. Never wire money to a personal rather than a business account. Preferably, use an escrow payment service such as PayPal or Moneybookers that will protect both parties' interests, or speak to your bank about wiring funds. But be aware these are hard to recall once the process has started.
- As a buyer, spread out payments if you can, and as a seller make sure you don't leave yourself exposed. You will have to negotiate with your partners to find a payment solution that is agreeable to both parties. Some people work on the basis of 30% payment before production begins, allowing final approval of samples before any more cash is paid. When it comes to final payments, some people ask for proof the full order has been produced, perhaps with a photo, or wait until the order has been dispatched. Remember, there is risk on both sides and some trust will have to be involved. This is why the due diligence process at the front end is so important ask for references, do a simple internet search for posts about the vendor/buyer in public forums and follow your instincts if something doesn't work for you and your business then choose a different avenue.
- Make the most of incentives for business growth offered by your local or national government funds are available for those entrepreneurs looking to actively grow their business. Now is the time to invest in your company, to make the most of the positive momentum for small/medium businesses in today's economic climate.

Exchange Rates

- As an example, in the UK, the depreciation of sterling has boosted exporters' prof its as firms have not passed all of the fall in the pound on to their buyers. This remains a good reason for firms to enter the UK export market. According to the Treasury, the corporate tax measures introduced in the emergency budget and the subsequent release of resources from the government should further support supply-side activity.

- Until recently China tied its own currency to the dollar however it no longer pegs its currency. As a result it is now more favourable for countries outside of the US to trade with China.

Security

- As you would when dealing with any new business contact, do some research. Check the background of the company. Are they members of a trade association or do they have any kind of verification/certification for the products they are developing? Do a credit check.
- Are they happy for you to speak to references? Beware of companies who just have a PO box or where the phone always goes to voicemail during the country's standard working hours bear in mind you may have to get up during the night to try this!
- **Keep paperwork clear** - spell out what you expect in terms of delivery and the product itself.
- **Beware fraudsters and scammers** - although a tiny proportion of people are untrustworthy, it pays to be sensible. If it sounds too good to be true, it probably is.

Transportation/Logistics

- If you are importing, your supplier is responsible for safely packing the order and completing the paperwork necessary to clear the port on their side of the transaction. If you are exporting then the responsibility is in your hands. The seller will usually get the product to a port and then the purchaser needs to organise shipping.
- Assuming this is going to be an ongoing arrangement, it makes sense to try and find transport partners you will be able to build an ongoing relationship with. Ask for quotes for shipping via sea and air and make sure they include all duties and fees involved, as these can have a sizeable impact to the end price of a product.
- If you are the buyer it is your responsibility to ensure the goods can legally be imported into the country and to get the products through customs.
- There is a wide range of shipping/duty terminology and acronyms you may need to familiarise yourself with as you go along - http://www.acronymfinder.com/ is a useful resource. And make sure you double check the small print.
- Ensure either you or your supply chain partner has insurance in place to cover the goods whilst they are in transit.
- Factor in the time needed to import/export and plan accordingly. Don't overpromise.
- You could consider working with an import/export professional to manage the process for you, especially if this is something you intend to start doing more frequently.

LeSports: ChannelAdvisor Makes Online Marketplaces Manageable

"We have settled all these channels with just one bit of software. It makes life so much easier."
-LeSports Director, **James McIlvenny**

www.lesports.co.uk
New Mills, England
Online Sportswear and Equipment

Overview
When LeSports was founded in 1980, the sportswear and equipment provider supplied independent sports retailers with the latest trends in sportswear. However, as the independent retailers dwindled due to the large sportswear chains moving in, LeSports changed its direction and moved to selling directly to the consumer. Even as its products moved to online stores like eBay and Amazon, LeSports never changed its mission statement: to supply quality branded sports clothing, footwear and accessories at competitive prices with excellent customer service.

Situation
Transitioning from supplying retailers to selling directly to consumers online was an extremely tedious process for LeSports. The marketing director of LeSports, James McIlvenny, explained, *"Prior to using ChannelAdvisor, we had no other solution in place. Everything was done manually. We had some staff members doing schedules and other staff carefully monitoring where products were best selling. It was very time-consuming."*

LeSports found it difficult to distribute and manage its inventory across its own webstore and multiple marketplaces. The company had no strategy for listing merchandise—they were listing the full inventory on eBay yet listing very few products on Amazon. The company also had difficulty managing orders as they were coming in from multiple sources —they needed a central platform from which to manage orders to track inventory properly.
"Amazon ran out of stock, eBay ran out of stock. We needed a solution to combine both channels into one—we could not manage the inventory," he said.
The sportswear and equipment provider stood at a crossroads with two options left: to fall at the feet of sportswear giants or revive its online resources with an e-commerce strategy.

11

Solution

LeSports implemented ChannelAdvisor's Premium Marketplace and Premium Webstore solutions to manage and distribute its inventory. Knowing that its retail client base was diminishing, e-commerce was flourishing and its ChannelAdvisor solutions were working, LeSports knew it was time to shift its sales entirely online.

The decision to use ChannelAdvisor came easy to McIlvenny; the technological experience and customer support capabilities were just what LeSports needed. LeSports, for the first time, had one place to monitor all inventories across multiple channels. Using the Inventory Juggler feature of ChannelAdvisor's Premium Marketplaces solution enabled LeSports to list inventory from a single source across eBay, Amazon and its own webstore. The Inventory Juggler feature tracks the inventory to make sure that if it sells out on eBay, it is not listed for sale on Amazon. This ensures that LeSports is no longer listing products for sale that are out of stock, improving the customer experience and LeSports' seller status.

LeSports also uses ChannelAdvisor's Premium Webstores solution. *"We were at a point where we had our marketplaces going well—we wanted to grow the business online,"* he said. Using ChannelAdvisor's Cross-Channel Dashboard LeSports can compare how products are performing on its webstore, eBay and Amazon and make performance-based product decisions. For example, if a product is selling particularly well on Amazon, LeSports can quickly shift inventory from eBay to respond to the demand.

Results

Since using ChannelAdvisor, LeSports has seen year-over-year growth of 49% on marketplaces, and is forecasting that the company's growth will continue. LeSports also anticipates continued growth on its webstore as the company works with ChannelAdvisor to develop the comparison shopping strategy and eventually a paid search strategy as well.

"With ChannelAdvisor our e-commerce strategy is completely automated so we spend no time at all on the tedious tasks of listing products online, reviewing product performance and chasing down orders and inventory to ensure that that we are not out of stock," McIlvenny said.
"ChannelAdvisor gives us more time to focus on our overall strategy and the ability to analyse and review product performance, too. Without ChannelAdvisor, we would probably need to recruit another two or three people purely to manage what the software is currently doing."

Due to its initial success with ChannelAdvisor, LeSports expanded its product availability to list items on eBay in America, Australia, France and Germany and more recently Amazon France. *"The inventory is shared,"* McIlvenny said, *"We have settled all these channels with just one bit of software. It makes life so much easier."*

Premium Marketplaces, Premium Webstores

ChannelAdvisor combines on-demand software, integration technology and best practices to help retailers manage the complexities of selling across multiple e-commerce channels - more efficiently and more profitably - all through a single interface.

A powerful part of the ChannelAdvisor platform, Premium Marketplaces helps retailers sell more and spend less on sites like Amazon, Buy.com, eBay, Pixmania and Trading Post. Allowing online retailers to focus on growing their business, Premium Marketplaces automates the tedious tasks of e-commerce from product distribution to post-sale. ChannelAdvisor's Webstore solutions make it easy for retailers to up-sell products from eBay stores to their own websites and cross-promote products over multiple marketplaces, effectively driving conversions, merging across-the-board efficiencies and extending retailers' brands to a broader audience.

To learn more download the video case study at www.channeladvisor.co.uk/ lesportsvideo

collect+

parcels made easy

The convenient and cost effective way to send your parcels to your customer's address.

The Collect+ service is quite simply the most convenient way for you to send your parcels to any address in the UK. As Collect+ uses convenience stores around the UK which are typically open early 'til late 7 days a week, you can drop your parcels off at a time that suits you. No more dashing to the Post Office before it closes or waiting in for a courier, the Collect+ service is in tune with how you run your account. Do you arrange most of your sales in the evening and weekends? No problem, just drop them off when its convenient for you and they will be collected next day.

That is why Collect+ is different and why it's the courier most suited to eBay users. We are open when you do your business - you don't have to work around restricted opening times & you don't have to wait in for collections. And there is a Collect+ convenience store near you!

You can arrange delivery to any address in the UK whether it's a work address or a home address. What could be easier? What's more, Collect+ customers are strong advocates of our service - in a recent survey, 95% would recommend the service to a friend.

With one of the simplest websites for booking a parcel and with highly competitive prices, it's simply the easiest way to ensure you and your customers receive the best service.

Use Collect+ and you enjoy all these benefits:

- Choose from over 3,500 convenience stores to drop your parcels off
- Most people live within 1 mile of a Collect+ convenience store
- All stores open early 'til late 7 days a week
- All parcels are tracked
- Simple, fixed pricing within the eBay shipping caps
- Meets the seller protection requirements
- Trusted by major direct retailers such as Littlewoods, Very, Bodens, ASOS, M&M Direct & House of Fraser

How it works
Booking a parcel and sending is as easy as 1 - 2 - 3!

1. Visit http://www.collectplus.co.uk and print your label. Its quick and easy to book a parcel for shipment - in fact our customers say the Collect+ web site is the simplest on the market
2. Attach your label to the parcel & take it to your nearest Collect+ convenience store (just enter your postcode and the convenience stores near to you will be displayed)
3. Relax and track your parcel on line. At each stage of the journey, your parcel will be clearly visible.

Alternative delivery options
Using Collect+ means you have the option of sending your parcels to another convenience store near where your customer lives. Ideal if your customer is out most the of the day and is worried about missing the delivery. If you choose this option, we'll even text your customer when it's arrived in store.

Simple and easy to understand pricing
Collect+ aims to make sending your parcels as easy and convenient as possible. This includes the pricing. All you need to do is to decide whether you are sending to an address or to another convenience store. After that there are only 2 price levels, upto 5kg, and over 5kg. That's it. Simple as that. Pricing is (as at Jan 2011):

Upto 5kg
Sending to another convenience store - £3.49
Sending to any address in the UK - £4.99

Over 5kg - £6.99
Included in the price at no extra cost
Not only are these prices very attractive, they automatically include:

- All parcels tracked as standard
- You receive a receipt as proof of despatch
- Insurance upto £50 (more available at additional cost)
- Customer service assistance if necessary

Linked to eBay
Your eBay account can also be linked to your Collect+ account. This enables you to automatically import your orders and download your addresses - meaning there is no need to re-type the customer's details.

Want to get started?
Visit http://www.collectplus.co.uk

dZine-Hub
Custom eBay Designs & Website Solutions

Give your eBay store the face-lift it needs with our *custom design*

dZine-Hub puts your eBay store on the map with a custom eBay store design & listing template design. At only £399, you can get your eBay store custom designed by us along with a matching listing template design to list your items with. Now seriously, why be ordinary when being exceptional is an option?

Consistent Branding - Get a state of the art eBay store design with a matching listing template design to achieve consistent branding!

WHY eBay store design & listing template design?

- **Branding -** Give your eBay store a top-quality design with a unique logo.
- **Interface -** Give your eBay store easily navigable pages that facilitate a shopping experience to remember for your visitors.
- **Cross-Promotion -** Creative methods of cross-selling & cross-promotion that makes the difference between a visit and a sale.

Advanced Features- Custom Add-ons:

- **Seasonal Themes**
  Eg. http://stores.ebay.com/PASHION

  We offer the provision for you to apply a theme on your eBay store for a holiday season during that period. You can have your eBay store custom themed for Christmas, Halloween et all. Once the particular season is over, we can switch it back to the general theme on the eBay custom store design.

- **Category Promotion Boxes**
  Eg. http://stores.ebay.com/skiwear4u

One of the successful methods of selling is cross-promotion. The best way to do this is to use category promotion boxes - we help you use your space effectively to cross-promote your main categories of items on the listing tem plate and the eBay store design.

- **Flash Rotator Banner**
  Eg. http://stores.ebay.com/FashionRepublicUK
  A picture speaks a thousand words - imagine if there were five! Get a dynamic XML based, fully customizable high-visibility flash banner rotating gallery to convey key information about your eBay store!

- **Flash header**
  Eg. http://stores.ebay.co.uk/GLITZYGIZMOS
  Enhance your custom eBay store design with a flash animation header to make it the eyecatching eBay store it could be! The same animated header could be used on your listing template design as well.

Features that come with the design package (on request)

- Dependent dropdowns to search items by gender, color category, etc These are part of the design package and can be included in the design.
  A buyers search is made easy with these dropdowns. Here are a few samples stores where we have implemented complex dependent/independent drop down boxes:
  http://stores.ebay.co.uk/Shoe-Dream
  http://stores.shop.ebay.co.uk/Shu-Crazy-4-Womens-Shoes-and-Boots
  http://stores.ebay.co.uk/ShoeFashionista1

Promotion boxes (unlimited)
For cross selling we can create any type of banners (vertical, horizontal, etc) and display your items, categories, featured items, etc in it. and also promotion boxes.

Here are some stores where we have incorporated promotion boxes in the design.
http://stores.ebay.co.uk/PASHION?_rdc=1
http://stores.ebay.co.uk/FashionRepublicUK?_rdc=1

- **Variation promo boxes**
  This is a store we designed with variation promo boxes
  http://stores.ebay.co.uk/shoedream

You will notice that each promo box contains a drop-down for color & size.

- **nXn Search Matrix- (laptopAid store design)**
  The laptop aid ebay store is pretty complex, and we may have to work a custom proposal for you in case you need a similar ebay store. The laptopAid ebay store was designed to use a 15 X 15 complex structure, to enables their customers to search across 15 brands vs 15 categories in each brand, and vice-versa.
  http://stores.ebay.com/LaptopAid

- **Drop down Menus**
  Simple vertical drop down menus on ebay, to display your custom store categories and sub-categories. Example of a store with drop-down menus:
  http://stores.ebay.com.au/grumpybwatertanks
  You will notice the header menu containing drop downs which is different from other rollover-menu stores. Based on your requirements such a header menu can be designed to enable better searching of your products.

- **Horizontal Large Menu- Header**
  This type of menu header is especially useful to display large number of categories & subcategories. On mouse hover, it displays, and disappears when user moves pointer to another location.
  Please view this store header where we have incorpo rated this feature :
  http://stores.ebay.co.uk/My1stWish

- **Search by price box**
  Give your buyers the option to search items not only by colour or size but also by a price range.
  You will find this feature on the right hand side in this store:
  http://stores.ebay.com/BrinZU/

- **Multiple Images Script**
  We have allowed for the users of our listing template to use multiple images with the listing template to better show-case their item. The images appear as thumb-nails, and when the mouse is hovered over the thumbnail images, the large image populates in the main image section. This can be made compatible even if the seller is using a seller listing tool.

A few of the listing tools we have configured the

18

multiple image module for (with examples):

Inkfrog: http://cgi.ebay.co.uk/190480808190
Channel Advisor:
http://cgi.ebay.co.uk/140490704779
Auctiva: http://cgi.ebay.com/110624206835
eSellerPro: http://cgi.ebay.co.uk/150507936376
Vendio: http://cgi.ebay.com/320631633225

WHY choose Dzine-Hub?
Four simple reasons that make Dzine-Hub the only choice –

- **Quality -** When you choose a design partner, choose wisely. Quality is the focus - a top quality design can encourage a sale, while an amateurish or no design might do otherwise. Actions speak louder than words - visit our website portfolio for the *"actions"*.

- **Service -** All your emails, queries and revisions are handled quickly and efficiently.

During the project phase.
We answer all emails within 24-36 hours on business working days (Monday - Friday). Our project managers are available on the phone for discussions for a time-slot, if scheduled to give you personalized support.

Customer Satisfaction is of paramount importance to us - we do not stop revising your design until we find that you are completely satisfied with it.

- **Pricing -** Our design & quality levels are second to none; we deliver nothing short of the best. And the pricing is no exception - at £399 it is the best you can get for the entire package.

- **Flexibility -** We do not have any monthly membership plans where a customer could be tied to use any seller tool that we may own. Rather, we customize the listing template to suit the seller tool of their choice like ChannelAdvisor, Inkfrog, Auctiva, BlackThorne, TurboLister, etc.

Interested? Contact sales@dzine-hub.com for more information or call us on **01614-083 726**

Garage Sale 6

http://www.iwascoding.com/GarageSale

Mac OS X users - create outstanding eBay auctions GarageSale is the most comprehensive eBay application optimised for use on Apple platforms. Whether you are using an Apple Mac computer, an iPhone, iPod Touch or your iPad, you can edit, track and manage all your auctions with one application. Auction tracking keeps you up to date with all the information about your eBay auctions including current bid, watchers and listing fees. When a listing ends you'll receive all the information you need including the buyer's name, and address. You can add them to your address book and even find the buyer's location through Google Maps as well as leave buyer feedback directly from GarageSale.

Full Apple integration is outstanding with features such as the Media Browser which lets you import photos from different sources easily. You can even access all your images from iPhoto and Aperture directly from within GarageSale.

If you use Apple platforms to run your business, whether that be Mac computer, iPhone, iPod Touch or iPad, than GarageSale is the solution you should be using.

GarageSale offers:

- A completely Mac based eBay selling solution
- Free image hosting for up to 20 images per auction
- No subscription required, one-time
- iPhone/iPad versions available, too
- Pricing from $39.99

GarageSale is a slick, full-featured client application for the eBay online auction system. With GarageSale Mac OS X users can edit, track and manage all their auctions with one single application - easily and fast. Use GarageSale's intuitive and reliable interface to create eBay auctions conveniently. Stop waiting for eBay to lead you through endless web pages step-by-step.

GarageSale is fast, easy to use and comes with everything you need to create, list and manage your auctions. GarageSale also integrates perfectly with iPhoto, offers free image hosting, over 140 free auction designs and comes with a built-in Design Store. eBay Stores, eBay Motors, PayPal, Twitter and many international eBay sites are supported.

GarageSale Touch and GarageSale HD offer all the features you need to list products onto eBay while you are on the road. You can even start creating your auctions directly from your iPhone or iPad and then import them into GarageSale for Mac to refine them further. You can download GarageSale for the iPhone or iPod touch directly from the Apple App store and there is a separate version of GarageSale in the Apple App store for the iPad.

GarageSale is fully featured with all the tools that you would expect including Inventory Tracking, Batch Editing, Revision, Relisting and Free Scheduling. Support for multiple eBay seller accounts and full integration with eBay stores is built in as standard. Each time you upload an auction you can choose which of your eBay accounts should be used. Each account can be linked to a different PayPal account.

One of the most useful features in GarageSale is Network Sharing - the ability to share your prepared auctions with other GarageSale users on your local network with Apple's Bonjour technology. Inventory Tracking allows you to now define products and assign product titles, pricing information, images, and quantity. You can link your auction templates or a variation from a variation-enabled listing with your product through the SKU field. Every time an item sells, GarageSale will decrease the remaining quantity for the linked product.

Built in to GarageSale is a Financial Report Geneator to enable you to stay in control of your business. It's crucial to your business success to keep track of your eBay income and expenses so GarageSale lets you create custom reports showing the data you are interested in, including PayPal and eBay fees, for any given date range.

What have other eBay users said?

- This is by far the most awesome app for eBay postings using a Mac. Not only is it powerful, but it is just plain FUN to use!
- Using GarageSale has been instrumental in starting my eBay business. It has worked flawlessly and makes beautiful listing designs seem effortless. The customer support is top notch.
- Quite easily the best eBay Auction manager, by a

country mile. Superb software.

- Can't fault it so far, much better than Turbolister.

Goofbay is an essential bargain hunting companion, whether you are buying, or selling on eBay. As one of the biggest eBay tools specialists on the web, Goofbay has grown quickly since being established in early 2005. Here, we take a look at some of the free tools on offer through Goofbay.

Free eBay Sniper

You've seen it before; your bid is winning as the eBay auction is about to close. You watch in excitement for the eBay winning notification, but...it never comes, you've lost?! In the last seconds of the auction a new bid has appeared, somehow they have managing to outbid you and it's too late for you to respond. You've been sniped!

If you're tired of losing eBay auctions Goofbay eBay Sniper is the answer. Goofbay's free eBay Sniper automates the process of placing a bid in the closing seconds of an eBay auction, dramatically increasing your chance of winning.

There is no complicated software to learn; all you do is enter the eBay item number and your maximum bid. Goofbay will snipe eBay just a few seconds before the auction ends, so you can rest easy knowing you have the best chance possible of winning the auction.

Thousands of buyers snipe eBay auctions every day, if you can't beat them - join them!

eBay Most Popular Tool

This tool allows users to view how popular an item is through the number of watchers it has achieved. With this information, eBay sellers can better understand pricing points and demand for items, whilst buyers can better understand what type of Best Offer a user may accept.

eBay Bid History Tool

The eBay Bid History Tool allows you to lookup what someone is bidding for on eBay. You can see what items they have won, the percentage of auctions they have the winning bid in and how much they have spent in anywhere up to the last 120 days.

eBay Seller History Tool

The eBay Seller History Tool allows you to view a seller's sale history. You can see exactly what a seller has sold, how many they sold, how much their turnover was and how much they spent in eBay fees in up to the last 90 days. The Seller History Tool is particularly useful for eBay Sellers researching which products are selling most effectively online.

eBay Feedback Checker

The eBay Feedback Checker Tool allows you to lookup the entire feedback history of a seller or buyer on eBay. You can filter out positive feedback, negative feedback, withdrawn feedback and neutral feedback, allowing you to easily see the reliability of the seller or buyer you are dealing with.

eBay Best Offers Tool

The eBay Best Offers Tool allows you to view what offers a seller has accepted or declined. You can see exactly how often a seller accepts an offer and the average reduction a seller will accept in up to the last 90 days. Use this tool to better understand how much you can expect a seller to accept on a Best Offer.

eBay Misspellings Search

The eBay Misspellings Search allows you to search for items that have been misspelled by the seller, giving you more chance of picking up a bargain as nobody else can find it. For example if you type in 'Playstation', Goofbay will automatically search for misspellings such as Paystation, Playstaion, Playtation, and more.

If you are searching for a new camera, why not use the advanced filters to filter results by Brand, Model, Zoom, Bundled Kit, Megapixels and more.

eBay Bargains Search

The Bargains search allows you to search for eBay items with zero bids in order of when the auction is ending. You can further refine this search to find specific items which immediate impulse bargains are waiting to be had.

eBay Not In Title Search

This is a totally unique feature, no other site searches this way. You search for example 'PSP Games' and Goofbay lists those games where people have excluded 'PSP' or 'Games' from the title. (Games listed in the PSP category with a title as '2 games' etc. usually go undiscovered on eBay).

eBay Exact Search

The eBay Exact Search allows you to do a regular search on eBay but has the benefit of using the Goofbay advanced search filters to quickly and easily find the perfect item. If you are searching for a new camera, why not use Goofbay's advanced search to filter results by Brand, Model, Zoom, Bundled Kit, Megapixels and more.

eBay Local Search

Use this tool to search for items that are local to you with the eBay Local Search tool. By searching for local items, it's possible to grab a bargain and save on delivery costs by collecting it the very same day.

eBay Impulse Search

The eBay impulse search allows you to quickly search eBay for auction items currently below their perceived auction value. For example, you can search for Xbox 360 related items for under £10. The impulse search allows you to uncover bargains on items you often never expected. If you've never used Goofbay before, now is the time to have a go with some of the tools. If you are one of the 100,000 people who currently use eBay, then why not take the opportunity to use a wider range of its tools to better identify eBay bargains. You could use tools in conjunction with one another, for example using the 'Not in Title Search' to identify a bargain, before using the Free eBay Sniper to stand the greatest chance of winning it?

In addition to these tools, Goofbay also offers a range of buyer and seller shortcuts, completing its offering as an essential eBay companion. The developers of the site are also looking to bring news of the latest eBay deals and bargain hunting opportunities as they happen. To receive the latest bargain hunting opportunities and for updates on new Free eBay tools, sign up to Goofbay now. You can also receive updates through joining http://www.facebook.com/goofbay, or follow Goofbay at http://www.twitter.com/goofbay_com.

Linnworks Order Management and Stock Control

Linnworks allows you to manage all your selling channels from one straight-forward software system. Whether you sell on eBay, Amazon, PlayTrade, Pixmania or your own website, you can manage your entire inventory from one place, ensuring that you'll never sell something you don't have in stock.

For example, when you sell an item on eBay, Linnworks will automatically deduct one from your available stock on Amazon. The system does it seamlessly for all your selling channels, making sure you never sell more than you can deliver.

With Linnworks, all your orders from multiple channels are downloaded into one central place, where you can print all invoices, shipping labels, picking and packaging lists at a click of a button, as well as keeping track of order life cycle and manage returns and resends.

Linnworks makes selling across multiple channels simple.

Order management
All your order management can be handled within Linnworks, removing the need to log into multiple websites and marketplaces. Centralised management takes care of everything from downloading orders, producing invoices and shipping labels and handling any returns or exchanges.

- Download orders from eBay all sites, Amazon all sites, PlayTrade, PixMania and many types of websites, including bespoke built e-commerce platforms;
- Print invoices, shipping labels, packing slips and pick lists for multiple orders at a click of a button;
- Automatically mark orders as shipped on your selling channels and upload shipping tracking numbers to update the order details;
- **Complete order life cycle** - product resends, returns, exchange and customer notes;
- **Email notification** - send out despatch notifications with PDF invoices attached, as well as create email

notifications for every step of the way;

Inventory Management

Inventory management is at the heart of Linnworks. It ensures that you have maximum exposure for your entire inventory but will never oversell when stock runs low as Linnworks will automatically adjust your stock profile on each marketplace as sales are made.

- One Inventory repository for all selling channels - there is no need to manage inventory for each SKU independently;
- **Stock level instantly updated on all your selling channels** - if you sell an item on one platform the quantity will be updated on the other marketplaces that you trade on;
- **Multiple listings/auctions can be linked to single product** - if you list the same item but in different quantities or with a different title it will still deplete stock from a single SKU;
- **Multiple stock levels for the same product** - this gives you flexibility to manage locations and multiple marketplaces;
- **Support for bundles, packs and composite products -** if you combine multiple products into a single bundle Linnworks can still automate your stock inventory for you;
- Stock Purchasing management as well as support for Just-In-Time ordering (ordering from supplier when orders are placed, instead of stocking internally);
- **Support for drop shipping** - if you use drop shipping services this can be integrated into your Linnworks management;

Shipping Integration (print labels from Linnworks directly)

With Linnworks all of your invoices, labels and shipping is taken care of from within the software. Linnworks integrates with the major shipping carriers and postal services to enable you to print out shipping labels without the requirement to cut and paste into the carriers own website.

- Royal Mail franking and Despatch Express integration
- Parcelforce
- FedEx
- UPS
- DHL and DespatchBay
- United States Postal Services (USPS)
- Interlink Express (shipping velocity)
- HDNL (shipping velocity)

Listing products

You can use Linnworks to create new listings on eBay, Amazon and Magento-based websites. Once you create an item in Linnworks you can then launch it onto multiple marketplaces and websites and Linnworks will ensure that the correct attributes for each marketplace are included correctly.

Terapeak for eBay - eBay Market Research for Sellers -
http://www.terapeak.com

Make more profit and close more auctions by using eBay market research.

Our sellers sell 65% more on average because they understand what prices buyers are historically willing to pay, what titles get found, and how to optimize their listings. Terapeak users sold a combined 4$ billion USD.

Successful eBay selling involves three things:

- Find the average price of an item, this is what buyers are proven to pay
- **Research your competition to see how they succeed -** the best sellers consistently sell 80% of their listings - learn from them and compete successfully
- **Optimize your listings based on what you find -** adjust price, change title key words to rank higher, close more listings

Research and identify the average price of your item:
Terapeak will show the dollar amount most buyers are proven to pay for something. Discovering this will make it much easier to price your items so as to maximize profit and avoid being passed over.

- Get the average sale price for your item and apply this value to your fixed-price listings or a lesser value to your bid auctions. Pricing your items effectively will entice buyers, you should avoid setting a price that is too high as these can quickly get passed over.
- Filter your search results appropriately compare vs. the tiem of year: be sure you are looking at a specific item and not the whole category's price - then compare the average price this time last year to know exactly what people paid (sometimes prices peak and you'll make more if you wait to list).
- Price your items using your new insight. Pricing is so vital to making a positive impact on buyers, remember, shoppers want bargains to jump out at them. Price your items fairly and customers will gravitate to your listings to make a purchase.

Find the top sellers and research competition:
Easily find the top sellers for your item(s). Finding them to review their listings will show you how to succeed; you'll see what listing styles are attractive to customers and what title key words rank highest and get found. Terapeak makes it easy to find all the following information quickly:

- Find the top sellers, Terapeak ranks top sellers for any item for you to look up and analyze. This is the foundation for building a successful listing, learning from the best.
- Review their listings to see what features, keywords and other listing elements they use. This is how you discover techniques that are proven successful.

A report will display
everything from pricing to a seller's most-successful day of the week - which you can immediately employ.

- Adapt your own listings to the successful style you find - until you do this you're not really competing. Remember there is a winning strategy to every item; fortunately uncovering it is fairly straightforward will tools like this.

Perfect your listings:
Use the proven listing features and techniques pulled from both a Terapeak item report and top sellers' listings to optimize your own listings. This is how you out-sell the top sellers.

- Time your listing, list when items are proven to sell - you need to find the optimal day and time to close your listings. Terapeak can easily show this and any seasonality (best time of year) your item has. End your listings at the exact time when shoppers are paying the most, this way you'll always maximize your end price.
- **Find the most searched keywords** - Terapeak's Title Builder will show valuable words that get the highest end price for an item, and popular words that searchers are already using. Listing as *"vintage"* vs *"retro"* can be the difference between a high price and a low price. You can know this ahead of time using Terapeak.

- Cover all your categories, many buyers search at a category level instead of a general search, be sure you use Terapeak to find every category your product should be in.

Terapeak will quickly tell you every category an item is listed in and how often it gets listed there and how often it sells. Remember we only show you closed listings, you are only ever looking at stats related to successful listings.

Finally, keep in mind that your listing appears shoulder to shoulder with all the others and it's easy for shoppers to move on. Listings that are priced well, with the right keywords and timed to perfection are assured to perform. Your best strategy is to employ the tools that give you this listing intelligence. The good news is that they're already at your disposal.

Go to http://www.terapeak.com/ for more information, good luck with your selling.

Overview
The only product of its kind within the UK, Tradebox Finance Manager is a unique accountancy plug-in solution for online retailers wishing to impose financial control over their trading activities. Designed as middleware, Finance Manager acts as an automated bookkeeping tool, importing completed orders from eBay, as well as a range of other online sales venues, and comprehensively accounting for each online order in Sage Instant, Sage 50 or Sage 200 accountancy solutions.

Features
In conjunction with Sage accounts solutions, Tradebox Finance Manager provides the online seller with a powerful package, enabling them to expediently:

- Import and process high volumes of online orders in minutes
- Drastically reduce data entry in Sage
- Create invoices/orders for each online order in Sage
- Create individual or generic customer records in Sage
- Map (matching and non matching) online SKU's to Sage stock codes
- Automatically calculate correct VAT liability for each individual online transaction based upon what has been sold and where it has been shipped to.
- Create and print invoices, labels and dispatch notes
- Create and print picking and packing lists
- Provide stock control
- Deal with combined 'packaged' items assembled from other stock items
- Upload adjusted stock levels back to the online sales

- channels
- Edit eBay SKU's (Custom Label Fields)
- Assess and reorder supplies
- Automatically create Purchase Orders in Sage for Drop Ship items
- Provide management information on product sales performance and profitability
- Provide analysis of sales channel performance
- Accommodate entry of direct sales
- Maintain an accurate financial account of the retailer's online sales

An overview of Finance Manager, containing prices, functionality and compatibility can be downloaded http://www.tradebox.uk.com/_assets/pdf/Finance%20Manager%20v4.5.pdf.

Benefits
For many businesses, dealing with the logistical requirements of processing, fulfilling and shipping mass orders can be extremely challenging. The ability to financially account for these sales, accurately and transparently is intrinsically time consuming, open to error and can be a significant barrier to growth.

With the ability to download, process and create financial entries in Sage Accounts for large volumes of online orders, in a fraction of the time it would take to do manually, Finance Manager can massively reduce the online retailer's administration burden and enable them to achieve further growth. By automating the creation of this financial information, Tradebox not only reduces duplication and time costs, it also removes inaccurate data inputs. In an environment where literally hundreds of individual invoices and customer records may be raised manually every day, this is can be a real danger.

- Saves money for retailers
- Dramatically reduces data entry time
- Streamlines post-sales administration
- 100% accurate
- Enables business growth

Assessment & Customer Reviews
Tradebox Finance Manager is available to download as a free, fully supported, 14 day trial for existing Sage users. The Tradebox Installation Guide and Checklist can be downloaded http://www.tradebox.uk.com/_assets/pdf/FM%20Installation%20Guide%20and%20Check%20List.pdf. This is a comprehensive step by step guide that provides guidance on:

- Essential Sage configuration prior to installing Finance Manager.
- Advice and recommendations on other Sage configuration

- Finance Manager download and installation instructions.
- How to download data from specific online platforms and any pre-requisites prior to importing sales data.

Tradebox also run a live online demonstration at 11am every Wednesday and Friday where prospective customers can see both Tradebox and Sage in action. This is a really good way to evaluate the impact Finance Manager can have on the online retailers business and assist them in deciding whether to make a purchase, or not. A place at the online demo can be booked via the Tradebox website or by visiting:
http://www.tradebox.uk.com/_assets/pdf/Finance%20Manager%20v4.5.pdf.

Independent customer reviews of the Tradebox Finance Manager software and support can be found at http://cgi6.ebay.co.uk/ws/eBayISAPI.dll?SolutionsDirectory&page=details&solutionId=1054.

Support

An 'out-of-the-box' solution, Tradebox Finance Manager can be installed, configured and ready to import sales from eBay within minutes, foregoing the need for any expensive onsite consultancy. A range of step by step guides are provided to customers and prospects to assist them in getting started.

Both pre and post sales support, for both prospects and customers, is accessible via the Tradebox helpdesk, which is available between 9am and 3pm on all working days via telephone and email; 0191 280 4025 or support@tradebox.uk.com.

System Requirements & Information

- Sage Instant Accounts or Instant Accounts Plus, v15 onwards.
- Sage 50 (Sage Line 50) Accounts, Accounts Plus and Accounts Professional
  (Financial Controller) V11 onwards.
- Windows XP Pro, Windows Vista, Windows 7.
- Import sales from:

  eBay
  Amazon
  Play.com
  ChannelAdvisor
  Magento
  EKM Powershop
  Shopcreator
  247 Topseller
  LiquidShop
  Shopify

Any other ecommerce website capable of exporting a compatible csv order file. Full specification details of the csv export file can be downloaded here http://www.tradebox.uk.com/_assets/pdf/csv_import_overview.pdf.

Tradebox are constantly developing native connections to new ecommerce platforms to enable integration 'out of the box'.

Company Background
An accredited and award winning Sage Developer and Sage Business Partner, Tradebox has an in-depth understanding of the functionality available within both Finance Manager and all Sage products. Working within the online retail market since 2005 Tradebox also has a comprehensive understanding of the online retailer's business practices, placing us in a great position to evaluate the online retailer's accountancy needs, advise on product selection and assist them in getting started. As a Sage Business Partner, Tradebox can also offer all prospective Sage customers 10% off all Sage purchases.

A company overview of Tradebox, including a customer case study, can be downloaded here http://www.tradebox.uk.com/_assets/pdf/csv_import_overview.pdf

Tradebox Introducer Scheme
The Tradebox Introducer scheme is an extremely straight forward, low maintenance programme designed to reward Tradebox partners and customers that recommend, promote and successfully introduce new customers to Tradebox. For more details visit http://www.tradebox.uk.com/_assets/pdf/Tradebox%20Introducer%20Scheme.pdf .

Contact Tradebox
Telephone: 0191 280 4025
Email: sales@tradebox.uk.com
Web: http://www.tradebox.uk.com

Alibaba.com Products and Services:

Alibaba.com's main product is its online business to business trading platform, www.alibaba.com, connecting more than 56 million small and medium businesses from more than 240 different countries and regions around the world. As part of its online sourcing platform, Alibaba.com offers the following products and services:

1. **Customized Sourcing:** A service on Alibaba.com where buyers' sourcing requirements are matched with the right suppliers.

   a. Buyers must be registered Alibaba.com Members and have posted a clear and detailed Request for Quotation Form (RFQ Form).

   b. Suppliers are matched based on their quotes, capabilities, product/ service quality, etc.

2. **Buying leads:** Post a buying lead to tell suppliers what you want to buy and watch the responses roll back in to you from relevant suppliers.

3. **TradeManager:** A real-time chat programme built into the Alibaba.com platform that allows buyers to communicate with suppliers from around the world. Features include real-time text translation to helpbreak down language barriers and capability to send product photos or files of any size to your trade partners.

4. **Trade alert:** If you want to be kept updated on a specific product category, you can customise your own Trade Alerts to receive free updates on the latest products, trade leads, buyer & supplier information sent direct to your email inbox.

5. **Highly customisable search functions:** Your product search can be as general or as focused as you would like it to be. Search by category or keyword and refine your results using these filters:

a. Location of supplier
b. Gold Supplier status
c. Specific product characteristics such as style, material, etc.
d. Factory Audited suppliers
    i. **Pre-Inspected Onsite**
    ii. Audited Reports accessible online for your review
e. **Business type:**
    i. Manufacturer (OEM service, Design service, Buyer label), trading company, distributor/wholesaler, agent, association

6. AliExpress: An e-commerce platform under Alibaba.com that offers smaller-quantity orders, instant online transactions, and an escrow service to protect buyers and sellers.

   While Alibaba.com focuses on larger quantity orders including prototype and custom manufacturing, AliExpress directly addresses the needs of businesses that need smaller quantities available for immediate shipment.

7. **Safe buying services:**

   a. Pay securely online via Escrow on Alibaba.com. The Escrow service on Alibaba is powered by Alipay.com, a leading third-party online payment platform from the Alibaba Group.

      Escrow allows you to pay securely online with out exposing your credit card details. You can also track delivery of your order and payment is only released to the supplier after you confirm you've received the order.

   b. PayPal is now offered on the AliExpress platform (www.aliexpress.com). Businesses will now be able to easily source goods through AliExpress using PayPal in their preferred local currency.

8. **Shipping services:** Through its alliance with UPS, AliEx press now offers users the key benefit of managing their shipping and tracking processes online via UPS shipping technology integrated into the AliExpress

platform, including the ability to print UPS shipping labels and request pick-up for their UPS packages all from within the AliExpress website.

᙭channeladvisor®

If you are producing results on eBay and Amazon in your native country, chances are that you have considered expanding beyond your local boundaries to capture the buying power of other countries worldwide.

First, a look at the global opportunity. As demonstrated by the chart below, the estimated compound annual growth rate (CAGR) for the European Union (EU) predicts that e-commerce will increase 19 percent per year until 2014. The US will account for an estimated 11 percent annual increase, with the rest of the world (mainly Asia Pacific) establishing a 29 percent average annual growth.

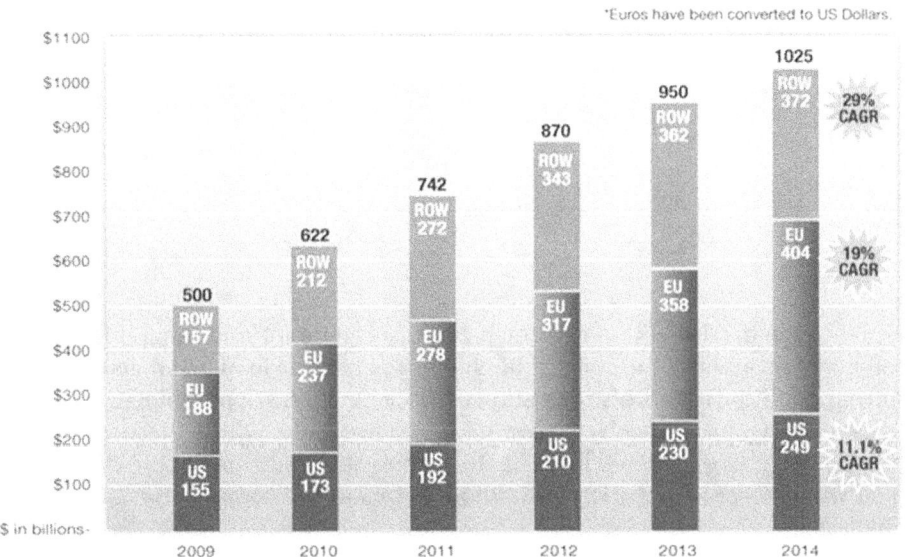

Source: US Department of Commerce, JP Morgan, ChannelAdvisor estimates , Forrester Research, IDC, eMarketer, UK eStats, TIA.org, and regional statistics bureaus.

For a deeper dive into the EU breakdown, the UK is the largest online spender, followed by Germany and France, which makes these countries logical targets for beginning an international e-commerce push.

EU-7 online retail sales per country
(€ millions*)

(€ millions)	2009	2010	2011	2012	2013	2014	CAGR (2009-2014)
UK	€24,739	€27,615	€30,573	€33,627	€36,760	€39,826	10%
Germany	€17,310	€19,099	€21,209	€23,275	€25,262	€27,156	9%
France	€9,376	€10,743	€12,236	€13,858	€15,488	€17,019	13%
Netherlands	€3,103	€3,525	€3,923	€4,342	€4,768	€5,155	11%
Italy	€2,521	€2,853	€3,212	€3,618	€4,078	€4,567	13%
Spain	€1,879	€2,295	€2,780	€3,337	€3,941	€4,571	19%
Sweden	€1,473	€1,681	€1,881	€2,074	€2,268	€2,444	11%

(numbers have been rounded)

Source: Forrester Research Online Retail Forecast, 1/10 (Western Europe)
*Data presented in 2009 constant euros

56543   Source: Forrester Research, Inc.

The language barrier with any foreign country can be intimidating, but that's really only scratching the surface of challenges to bear in mind when expanding internationally. There's also tax and currency considerations, shipping, customer service and much more to take into account. Whilst there is not enough space here to delve into the intricacies, the following abbreviated guide will give you a holistic view of how to tackle the complexities of global expansion.

Things To Think About	Companies to Talk To
Financial & Legal	

• Tax/VAT & Reporting
• Payment & Banking
• Local regulations
• Registering your business
  o Do you register locally?
• Import taxes/VAT: buyers may be charged one or both when buying from outside of Europe; the only way to legally bypass this issue is to import the goods yourself, thus either have a branch in the EU or use a fulfillment service
	• World First
	• PayPal
	• Local Banks
	  o Challenges with local banking include language barriers, regulations, as well as many require local addresses to register an account; Ask your home bank for a referral
	• MoneyBookers

Shipping & Fulfillment	

• Shipping times
• Returns
  o Are they accepted/ required?
  o What is the timeframe?
  o Are the returns coming in to a localised address?
• Delivery costs
  o Passed on to the consumer?
  o Absorbed?
  o Is order tracking included?
  o Signature required?
• Email Communications (Touch Strategy)
  o Order acknowledgment
  o Registration
  o Dispatch
  o Delivery delays, etc.
• Text Message alerts
  o Dispatch
  o Delivery Date confirmation
• What delivery options are available/offered/ preferred?
	• Amazon FBA (UK, FR, DE)
	  o Returns with FBA have to be sent to a local address, which then have to be picked up by a freight broker; This is time consuming and costly, and can be hard to manage reliably
	  o Non-EU customers will have to import the goods first
	• Third-Party Fulfillment/ Management Companies (Local/International)

Content & Pricing	
• Website currency conversions o Lack of localisation in terms of currency could cause issues • Website/Marketplace content translations o Unprofessional translations and incorrect use of key terms can cause bounce rates, loss of potential customers, inability to challenge local competitors in a particular market	• Translation services through companies such as: o Intercultural Elements o Language Wire o In-house translators
Customer Service	
• Timely customer communications in the local language are essential for successful retailer/client interactions and feedback o Do not cut corners with software-based translator tools at the expense of customer satisfaction	• Hire native-speaking staff on hourly basis to take care of customer enquiries • Provide good FAQs to avoid lengthy correspondence/ many-customer queries • For on-the-fly translations use real translators through a service such as: o Language Wire

In conclusion, if you already have the product and the infrastructure in place, selling internationally is a natural progression to grow your business and sell more. Be sure to plan carefully and only use reputable partners. Also, remember that the more shipping and payment options you can support, the less basket abandonment you'll encounter. Finally, eBay and Amazon are great places to start your international expansion, but don't forget about other channels, such as paid search and comparison shopping, that can be equally rewarding.

To learn how you can go global with ChannelAdvisor, visit www.channeladvisor. co.uk/goglobal or email go-global@channeladvisor.com.

channeladvisor®

"Not only does our new store look great, but within one week of launch the percentage of our overall turnover that flowed through it increased from 11% to 32%! It's great to have all of our channels managed under one roof - it allows us to focus more time on diversifying our sales from a traditionally eBay-centric approach as well as on sourcing new products. We are happy to report our Premium Store has exceeded all expectations."
-Mark Sharples, *Managing Director, Mekasa.co.uk*

An Opportunity to Reinforce Your Brand and Business
A webstore is not only one of your main outlets for selling product; it also serves as a hub for your brand. At the root of any well-balanced e-commerce strategy is a well-designed webstore that caters to the buyer, creating a user-friendly shopping experience that will increase conversions and, in turn, acquire repeat customers.

Now more than ever it is crucial to have an e-commerce partner with a scalable solution that can help you Sell More not only through your webstore, but also through key online channels.

Is Your Webstore Designed to Sell More?
ChannelAdvisor's Premium Webstores solution allows you to build your dream webstore to enhance the shopping experience on your site, grow your brand, optimise for search engines and boost conversions. With ChannelAdvisor's Inventory Management, you'll also be able to manage your inventory and orders across your Webstore and other e-commerce channels from one central platform, allowing you to expand your business without the hassle of trying to manage your inventory through several different interfaces and tools.

Premium Webstores uses an easy-to-navigate, secure, one-page checkout that minimises basket abandonment. No longer will customers desert shopping baskets because your checkout was too confusing or lengthy.

Mobile is on the Rise - Are You Missing Out?
With ChannelAdvisor's Premium Webstores solution you can launch a full-featured mobile version of your site in days without having to design a new, separate site. Our integrated platform does the work for you and automatically creates a store rendered to fit any mobile smartphone, so you never miss out on an opportunity to Sell More. Like your Premium Webstore, your Mobile Webstore's checkout is also designed to reduce basket

abandonment by being mobile-optimised to accelerate purchases on mobile devices.

Take Your Strategy to the Next Level through Performance-Driven Decisions In addition to a well-designed, effective Webstore and the advantages of Inventory Management, ChannelAdvisor's retail analytics give you the ability to create customisable reports that provide the insight you need to make performance-driven business decisions down to the product level.

You can view data by date, week, month or quarter comparing sales and trends across your Webstore and marketplaces such as eBay. You can also keep track of your profits and losses through detailed sales history reports, gather information on the recent sales (past 2 weeks) of each product and receive an estimate of how long the existing inventory will last.

For more information about ChannelAdvisor's Premium Webstore Solution go to http://www.channeladvisor.co.uk/premiumwebstore

Nothing is impossible - That is our attitude to eBay and website design.

Our designs are intuitive, funky and completely bespoke. No two are alike, our designs are unique. We offer integrated cross-selling, optimised user experience, multiple languages, product filters and many more features, even for your eBay shop!

We offer other business related services such as marketing, social media,corporate and brand design, managed service/fulfillment and ad-hoc business consultancy.

UK website: http://www.createyourtemplate.co.uk

eBay Shops:
We have developed exceptional technologies that allow us to establish your presence on eBay with a new or existing corporate design. Our eBay shop designs and eBay templates offer you all the features that you would expect from an advanced online shop. Your customers get a first-class shopping experience.

Online shopping is no longer a secret world!

Traditional businesses are seeing the potential of online sales. E-commerce has increased significantly as buyers become smarter and price compare online. Your business needs to be a part of it, let us help you get online!

Case Studies:
Grandstand Merchandise.

A brand new business, we had an idea and logo provided by the client and they needed a solution to work with their fulfilment and back office processes. We delivered and integrated a solution using Channeladvisor to serve eBay as well as an e-commerce website. Both eBay and website have dynamic upsells, focused banners, tailored product filters and searches. This new business will go from strength to strength with our design and support.
http://www.grandstandmerchandise.com
http://stores.ebay.co.uk/grandstandmerchandise

Passion4italianfashion

With a warehouse full of cutting edge fashion, passion4italianfashion needed a professional, stylish appearance on eBay. They only wanted the best so they chose Createyourtemplate to create their look and feel from scratch. Sporting a new, retro urban look with brand focus and body shape filters, passion4italianfashion will carve a new path in 2011!

http://stores.ebay.co.uk/passion4italianfashion

TackleDiscounts

Fed up and limited by his old eBay design, tacklediscounts needed a change on eBay. With a brand new fresh look and customer experience, his sales and basket value increased off season with his new design by createyourtemplate. His design is dynamic with banner advertising, product searches and three layers of cross selling.

http://stores.ebay.co.uk/TACKLEDISCOUNTS-ultimate-value

Yakuza Outlet Store

Yakuza is a cutting edge urban fashion brand and brought its outlet to eBay through createyourtemplate. Managing the design, implementation and fulfilment, the Yakuza brand is making its mark on eBay. This eBay shop integrates colour finders, intensive upselling and cross selling as well as pushing the savings!

http://stores.ebay.de/yakuza-outlet

cytSEO

Search engine-friendly programming is a matter of course with our online shops. We also offer our clients enhanced services concerning search engine optimisation.

Be found easily with your keywords with our SEO tool, the perfect alternative or compliment to pay per click. You determine the keywords, the description and our technology does the rest.

Branding

As a creative agency, we offer you the perfect blend of e-commerce advice and branding. For our clients without an existing corporate design, the development of a credible, contemporary and professional design is a long-term commitment to their public image.

dZine-Hub
Custom eBay Designs & Website Solutions

eBay Bulk Listing Services:

What:
We have uploaded tens of thousands of items for our clients who supply the product information either in the form of a spreadsheet or simply point us to a supplier website and we add all the products from a supplier website, to their ebay store.

Here are a few examples:
http://stores.shop.ebay.com/Plexsupply (bulk uploaded over 20,000 items)
http://stores.ebay.co.uk/AdventureNorthumberland (Created a clone of their supplier website- www.cyclelife.com, and bulk uploaded the same products in their ebay store), etc.,

We provide specialized eBay Bulk Products Listing services to automate the task of listing your items on eBay.

- Optimize item titles to make them eBay friendly
- Keyword stuff item titles and ensure they are under 55 characters in length
- Setup store categories on ebay
- Map the ebay store categories with your product inventory
- Map each inventory item to a relevant eBay category
- Converting your custom inventory spreadsheet into an ebay bulk upload format
- Upload the products in batches of 500 or 1000 to your ebay account, depending on your total inventory size

Ensure that everything is setup perfectly!

Why:
Bulk uploading items saves time which you would have spent to list your items

and allows you to concentrate on running your business instead.

http://www.dzine-hub.com/spending-time-uploading-items-ebay-store/

- Do you have over 100,000 items to upload to ebay?
- Do you want to upload 50,000 items in 3 days?
- How can you manage over 50,000 items in your ebay inventory?

How:
If you Have a website, we can launch an ebay store with the product feed from the website.

Yahoo store owners can export the product feed from their existing websites. Same with
customers using ANY ecommerce application like bigcommerce, xcart, magento, cubecart, etc can export the product feed in a flat file like CSV or XML. We can take that, and create ebay listings in bulk. Or, point us to supplier website (like www.bookdepository.co.uk) and we gather all the information from the suppliers/manufacturer's website to create your identical ebay listings.

The tools we use for our bulk upload process are:
- Turbo Lister
- File Exchange
- Selling Manager
- Blackthorne
- Selling Manager Pro
- In-house developed tool to automate listing, scheduling, etc.

Have more questions?
Contact sales@dzine-hub.com for more information or call us on 01614-083 726

dZine-Hub
Custom eBay Designs & Website Solutions

eCommerce Website Design:
Sell on your website with the same matching theme as your ebay store!

What:
We provide custom theme-based solutions for xcart, cubecart, zen cart, magento, cscart, bigcommerce, etc.

Magento + m2epro plugin- Offers excellent multi-channel selling capabilities (ebay & website only). A good alternative for tools like CA, vendio, zoovy, infopia, prostores, etc. who charge monthly + transaction fees. And we offer magento theme design, which of course would match your ebay design to maintain brand consistency and fully educate our clients to manage their ebay-website inventory from one place.

Advantage of magento+m2epro based websites:

- **No monthly/recurring charges** - open source
- Manage your entire website + eBay inventory from one interface
- Easy to work with & saves time
- Automatic update of inventory in ebay and website

WHY?

- Own your shopping cart software by option for an open source solution.
- Consistent branding of your business online - Your web site and eBay store would have a matching design.
- No listing fees.
- No final value fees.
- List as many items as you want.

A few websites we have designed:

http://www.kdirect.co.uk/
http://www.dgtalloys.com/
http://www.buildfind.com.au/

Matching ebay stores:

http://stores.ebay.com/Build-Find-Store
http://stores.ebay.co.uk/K-Direct-Limited
http://stores.ebay.co.uk/DGTWHEELS-TYRES

Interested? Contact sales@dzine-hub.com for more information or call us on 01614-083 726

To view the eCommerce Website Features Offered please visit
http://www.dzine-hub.com/ecommerce-website-design/

Frooition are a leading Certified Provider specializing in eBay design, with offices across the UK and US.

The main objective of Frooition eBay design is to increase traffic and grow your sales whilst saving you time!

Frooition currently offer two eBay design services: Advanced and Top Seller.

The advanced eBay design package is suitable for established eBay sellers and sellers who are just beginning to build their brand on eBay.

The top seller package is aimed at more established sellers who need to stand out in a competitive marketplace. They also need additional functionality to aid navigation through their inventory.

Advanced eBay Design
The solution includes custom branding based on the customers specific requirements. Frooition create a dynamic eBay storefront design and listing template. The storefront and listings have dynamic categories that can be automatically updated whenever you add or remove store categories - saving you hours of unnecessary work!

For live examples please visit:
http://frooition.com/uk/clientportfolio.html?cr=TamebayDirectory

For additional information please visit:
http://www.frooition.com/uk/serviceoverview.html?cr=TamebayDirectory

Top Seller eBay Design
The top seller eBay design takes all the fantastic functionality from the advanced eBay design and adds extra design options and additional functionality.

Customers also have the choice of some great, eye-catching, functionality such as iPad/iPhone compatible scrolling image panels that really dominate the look of the store!

For examples and to see what else is included please visit:
http://www.frooition.com/uk/ebay_top_seller.html?cr=TamebayDirectory

Design Management Software

In addition to the eBay design customers also get access to the online design management software.

The software enables customers to generate HTML templates, create templates for 3rd party listing tools (such as ChannelAdvisor & Vendio), or list directly to eBay. The software has many other features including the unique ability to instantly add the design to live listings in bulk saving hours of work!

The software allows customers to edit live listings; change titles, descriptions and prices in bulk!

Users can Tweet & Facebook links to your live items as well as setting up a FREE Facebook store!

For more information please visit:
http://www.frooition.com/uk/designmanagementsoftware.html?cr=TamebayDirectory

Ecommerce website design

Frooition offer brand matching design for ecommerce websites.

Built on the Powa store format, the ecommerce sites offer eBay sellers a great way to build an off eBay presence. The websites allow users to upload a spreadsheet of products as well as eBay integration.

For more information:
http://www.frooition.com/uk/powa_store_design.html?cr=site

Facebook fan page design: Frooition create completely custom Facebook fan pages designed to drive traffic directly to stand alone websites. The pages also encourage people to *"like"* your page and build momentum.

Facebook store design: Frooition have developed a unique storefront for Facebook pages.

It automatically displays your eBay inventory within your Facebook putting your products in front of hundreds more customers!

For more Facebook design information please visit:
http://www.frooition.com/uk/facebook_design.html?cr=TamebayDirectory

Other Frooition services include:

- ChannelAdvisor Premium Web Store design
- Vendio Web Store design

Visit http://www.frooition.com and register your interest to discuss your requirements today!

Don't forget to look for our discount code in the discounts section of this directory!!

myHermes is the perfect shipping partner for eBay sellers.

About myHermes
myhermes.co.uk is part of the UK's largest home delivery network and is the cheapest three to five day parcel delivery service in the UK. Ordering is simple and completed online, with door to door collection and delivery taking place through a network of local couriers.

Since its launch in 2009, myhermes.co.uk has had more than 1 million visits to its website and was listed by moneysavingexpert.com as the Best Buy for UK Delivery (items under 5kg).

Perfect eBay 'Economy' 4-6 day solution
eBay UK have standard shipping classifications, so that every time you send something it will be classified into Economy (4-6 days) / Standard (2-3 days) or Express (Next Day).

myHermes.co.uk has the perfect Economy 4-6 day solution –saving you time, money and improving your customer satisfaction, here's how...

> **myHermes** - makes delivery easy
> myHermes.co.uk operates with a keen focus on 'making delivery easy'.
> Customers are able to choose the day of collection up to 7 days in advance, track parcels online throughout their journey to the customer and the courier will even make three delivery attempts.

This helps to avoid the dreaded red card and the hassle of arranging a suitable time to drive to the sorting office to collect.

No more unhappy customers
myHermes.co.uk also recognises that a busy lifestyle does not always mean you can wait in for a parcel to be collected. A safe place option (that can be defined when registering) gives you the flexibility to carry on with your day as usual with the peace of mind that your parcel will be collected safely without you being at home.

This also works when delivering a parcel too; ask your customer for their safe place and we'll make sure we deliver it there safely if they're not in.

Save 70% of your time on eBay with myHermes

myHermes.co.uk's time saving feature 'Multiple Address Uploads' enables you to link your myHermes account to your eBay seller account to seamlessly transfer your completed listings to your myHermes shipments. This means the days of manually entering delivery details each time you need to send a parcel are long gone!

myHermes.co.uk revealed that out of 200 of its customers, almost three quarters said the function would save them up to half the time when sending parcels and another 15 per cent said it would save up to 70 per cent of their time.

Easy to use website

The website is simple and easy to use with a clear sequence from registration to ordering a parcel collection, simply register and tell them what you want to send and where along with weight and contents. Then just pay, print the label off and a courier will arrive on the selected day to collect the item from your home. You can then track the item online - it really is that simple!

There are helpful videos and pdf guides at www.myhermes.co.uk to help you get started.

Tradebox

Sage Software Overview

Managing your day-to-day finances, keeping track on what goes in and goes out, keeping on top of what's in stock and dealing with things like profit and loss isn't the most attractive part of running a business. However, having this function in house gives you an immediate and direct window into the health of your business. It puts **you** in control!

Want to know at a glance where your money is, what's due, what's overdue and what's expected? What products are in stock, what's on order and what kind of gross profit your products are returning? The Sage 50 Accounts 2011 range has all the tools to help you **make the right choice**.

Sage 50 Accounts 2011

Specially designed for small and growing businesses, Sage 50 Accounts helps you manage your customers and suppliers and day-to-day finances, including VAT returns, stock control, invoicing and year-end accounts. Because it's easy to use you can stay in control of your finances and share information with your accountant easily, giving you more time to run your business.

Key features

Cash flow
See how much you're making, what's due, what payments you need to make and what's already been banked

- **VAT returns**
  Fully accredited by HM Revenue & Customs so you can

prepare and submit
VAT returns online

- **Customers and suppliers**
  Match your customer and supplier info to quotes, in
  voices and communications, including details of
  deposits, discounts and credit

- **Stock Control**
  Comprehensive inventory of all stock, including
  quantity available in stock, suppliers, VAT liability, cost
  price, sales price, bar codes, locations

- **Reports**
  From an instant overview to the detailed facts and
  figures that help you understand your business
  Sage RRP from £560 (+VAT),
  Tradebox price from £504 + VAT

- **Sage 50 Accounts Plus 2011**
  Sage 50 Accounts Plus 2011 features all of the benefits
  of Sage 50 Accounts 2011 with additional tools to help
  you control your stock, manage individual projects and
  create custom pricing for different customers. It helps
  you manage everything from cash flow and VAT returns
  (including online) to year-end accounts, customers and
  suppliers while offering advanced reporting and budget
  management.

Additional Key features

- Tools to assemble products from other stock items - Bill
  of Materials (BOM)
- Early warning' stock Re-order levels and re-order
  quantities
- Individual customer price lists
- Project costing and management

Sage RRP from £810 (+VAT), **Tradebox price from £729 (+ VAT)**

Sage 50 Accounts Professional 2011

With Sage 50 Accounts Professional you can do more than just manage your
day-to-day finances. It also provides complete sales and purchase order
processing, alongside stock control project management and foreign trading
tools, so you can keep track of different areas of your business. With the
flexibility to handle up to ten users and help you manage multiple companies,
it gives you the information you need to drive your business forward.

Additional Key features

- Up to 10 users at a time
- Foreign trading and currency tools
- Sales Order Processing (SOP)
- Purchase Order Processing (POP)

Sage RRP from £1,095 (+VAT), **Tradebox price from £985 (+VAT)**

An accredited and award winning Sage Developer and Sage Business Partner, Tradebox has an in-depth understanding of the functionality available within all Sage products. Working within the online retail market since 2005 Tradebox also has a comprehensive understanding of the online retailer's business practices, placing us in a great position to evaluate the online retailer's accountancy needs, advise on product selection and assist them in getting started.

As a Sage Business Partner, Tradebox can also offer all prospective Sage customers 10% off all Sage purchases. A company overview of Tradebox, including a customer case study, can be downloaded here.

Contact Tradebox
Telephone: 0191 280 4025
Email: sales@tradebox.uk.com
Web: www.tradebox.uk.com

WebInterpret is an innovative software company which has been operating since 2007.

As an eBay developer program member, WebInterpret's goal is to increase the international sales of over 1,000 eBay sellers. WebInterpret delivers services to clients throughout Europe, North America and Asia.

WebInterpret enables you, among other things, to:

- **List your items Internationally within Minutes**
  All the listings you select can be automatically listed on multiple eBay sites (eBay.com, eBay.de, eBay.co.uk, eBay.fr, ..) with the appropriate modifications:

- The shipping costs for each country are automatically copied from the international shipping costs specified by you in the original listings

- All prices are automatically converted to the appropriate currency

- Our specially developed matching tool then places your items in the correct categories (eBay categories vary from country to country so it's important to make sure your listings appear in the correct ones)

- **Be understood worldwide with the help of professional translations**
  Your listings are accurately translated by professional translators.
  WebInterpret works with a large community of professional translators who have been carefully selected and trained to work on eBay listings (vocabulary, best practices, ...)

- **Appear in the top positions on foreign eBay sites**
  We train all our translators specifically on the eBay platform and, because we provide them with tools to select best keywords, your foreign listings appear at the top of the search results on each eBay site. This enables customers to find you directly on their local

eBay sites and buy from you with confidence.

- **Save time as we handle everything**
  At WebInterpret, our mission is to be as efficient as possible when it comes to expanding your global sales. To achieve this goal, we are proactive in handling all issues related to

  Internationalization:
- We automatically set up all the details on your foreign listings (currency conversion, shipping costs, stock synchronization, ...)

- You carry on using eBay in exactly the same way you are used to, you simply receive an email when you make a sale abroad. You can then continue to manage your sales on your eBay account as usual!

- We can duplicate and update in real time all or part of your UK eBay store to the eBay sites of your choice

- Get your stock automatically updated worldwide
  When an item is sold abroad on a foreign eBay site, available quantities are automatically updated and items are automatically removed if sold out from all the other eBay sites in real time.

  This way you are sure to avoid selling the same item twice.

If you have any question at all, we would be delighted to hear from you.

Please don't hesitate to contact us by email at info@webinterpret.com, or by phone on 020 7100 2262.

You can also try our solution for free by visiting our website:
http://www.webinterpret.com

advansys
ecommerce solutions

Be where shoppers shop

Advansys create award winning ecommerce solutions that can be scaled to give you a global presence with our multi lingual and multi currency modules. The biggest headache for most retailers is managing their multiple channels: eCommerce, telephone, retail shops, and marketplaces such as eBay, Amazon, Priceminister and Fnac. The Advansys framework takes this pain away by providing one single view. Instead of producing a number of complicated spreadsheets to be manually syndicated out to the multiple channels the Advansys framework simply allows you to assign the products to the appropriate channel within one intuitive interface. Stock levels are held centrally where the Retailer has full visibility with the ability to book stock 'in and out' and set minimum stock level values resulting in stock levels to be automatically replenished across all marketplaces.

Advansys Services:

- Global eCommerce Solutions

- eBay Store Designs
- Cross Channel Solutions
- mCommerce Solutions

Advansys
Building 4, Millars Brook, Molly Millars Lane, Wokingham, Berkshire. RG41 2AD
Email: sales@advansys.com
Website: http://www.adavnsys.com
Tel: +44 (0) 845 838 2700

Packing Partner is the fastest and smartest way to print labels, invoices and picking and packing lists. At the click of a button you can collect your sales records from sites such as eBay, Amazon, Play, osCommerce, Actinic and EKM and instantly print out VAT or non-VAT invoices.

As well as collecting the sales records Packing Partner will correctly format addresses and the invoices you print can include graphics as well as text. By using integrated labels with a peel off label you can print out your invoices and labels in a single process and even include an automatically selected Royal Mail printed post impression on your labels.

Packing Partner can also save you money by automatically combining orders to a single address. It can save you time producing invoices and Packing Partner can even mark items as dispatched once the sales records are collected and produce an export file for Sage or Quickbooks to make your accounting simple.

Packing Partner Invoice edition is £119.95, the Label Edition at £69.95 has many of the same features but prints labels and not invoices.

Watch the video on the Packing Partner website to see how to eliminate cutting and pasting of delivery addresses and produce professional invoices and labels with Packing Partner.

As Was is uniquely poised to improve your business through services that make you and your listings more memorable, generating more sales and more repeat business. Our average client sees a sales increase of 30% within weeks of finishing a project with us.

- We have been designing websites since 1995, and we pioneered eBay design and consulting in 2001.
- We are always innovating designs and layouts that are designed to cater to how eBay shoppers naturally think and behave.
- We're eBay experts who know and follow all the eBay rules. We guarantee eBaycompliant work.
- All of our staff are in the US and UK. Nobody is a *"junior"* staff member, and we don't use call centres.
- Our contract details that you own your design, and you can have your files.
- We never take a monthly fee or percentage of sales.
- You don't have to use our software. We can work with Auctiva, inkFrog, SellerSourceBook, CΛ, Kyozou, Black thorne, and others.

As Was can take care of anything your business needs to launch and grow including logo design, website design/development, print and promotional work, marketing, and sales strategies.

Contact us today for a free consultation to find out what we can do for your new or existing eBay business.

Say 'hello' to Bitsy

The friendliest business-to-business marketplace on the web Here at Bitsy, we think that you should concentrate on being the best eBay seller you can be. Do what you do best, we say. Outsource the rest!

So, whether you're looking for someone to take care of your bookkeeping, marketing or design, we can put you in touch with the right people to help your business grow.

And while we're at it, we can help you in other ways too:

- Through our small business blog with tips and advice on sales, IT efficiency, productivity and motivation
- Facebook-like social networking features that allow you to find help and support, add friends, create and join group
- And our B2B marketplace, a low-cost way to sell your services and outsource the skills to help you grow your business

What makes Bitsy special is its friendly community of small business owners - on hand to help, when you need it, or to hang out, when you need a break. It's free to join Bitsy and costs just £5 per month to list one service in the marketplace or £8 per month to list up to five.

Find out more at http://bitsythis.com

Froo Productivity Apps

All the Froo! Apps have free trials, sign up at http://apps.ebay.com

Froo have 4 eBay apps available from inside the eBay applications centre*;

Froo! Template Themes - $3.95 per month
Choose from over 4,000 professional eBay listing templates and apply them directly to your live listings! Get great looking listings instantly! Choose different templates for different listings.

Froo! Bulk Revision - 25 revisions a month for free
Save time and money when altering your eBay listings, no longer will you have to relist all your items to make changes to your listings, or if eBay make policy changes. Keep your listings up to date and manage your items more effectively. Froo! Cross Sell - FREE!

Add a FREE, sliding, cross promotion gallery to all of your live listings and offer your customer more choice! Choose a design to surround the gallery and promote up to 50 items on each listing.

Offer more products to more customers and sell more online!

Froo! Smart Social - FREE!
Froo! Smart Social is a completely free application that enables you to Tweet and Facebook your live eBay items. Either post in bulk or setup advanced automation rules to ensure you have a constant stream of links on your social network. Drive Facebook and Twitter traffic directly to your eBay items!

For more information please see http://www.froo.com

Please note the eBay apps centre is only available on eBay.com for eBay Motors, eBay US and Hong Kong users.

With InterCultural Elements, expanding internationally is elementary

InterCultural Elements helps your online business to grow domestically and internationally by expanding your sales to new markets. From marketplace advice over translations to technical conversion of your listings, we offer an A-Z solution which will enable you to grow your business substantially and diversify your risks.

Our services include:

- Translations of websites and product listings
- Create Ready-to-list Upload sheets for domestic and international market places such as eBay, Amazon, Pixmania, Buy.com, Price Minister, etc.
- ChannelAdvisor posting account setups & marketplace integration
- Marketplace & Website consultancy (e.g. how to in crease the visibility of your products)
- Marketplace strategy & statistical sales analyses

Whether you are looking to add language options to your website, expand your listings into foreign countries via eBay, Amazon and Pixmania or simply boosting your sales through a strategy analysis, we are the right partner to take you through the process while limiting your time investment to a minimum.

InterCultural Elements
Weissestrasse 5
04299, Leipzig
Germany:
Phone: +49 341 86382942
info@intercultural-elements.eu
www.intercultural-elements.eu

SellerExpress.com

SellerExpress is a low cost solution which manages your inventory, auto re-pricing and orders on PlayTrade, Amazon UK, France, Germany, USA, Canada and Japan (eBay available April 2011). No commissions and no long term contract. A 30-day free trial is available for a limited period. Sign up today at www.sellerexpress.com

sellernet.co.uk

SellerNet.co.uk

SellerNet is an enterprise level multi-channel application which allows you to sell on PlayTrade, Amazon UK, France, Germany, USA, Canada, Japan, FNAC, Priceminister, eBay.co.uk, eBay.com and your own website (including Rovi data). A powerful warehouse management system is also included. SellerNet also has a sophisticated bricks and mortar retail management and EPOS system. We have a wealth of experience in integrating SellerNet with 3rd party systems and developing bespoke functionality.

More info is available at www.sellernet.co.uk or call Brendan on 02871367730

PackVERTISE - the affiliate network for package inserts and print coupons

The **PackVERTISE network** connects advertisers and online sellers, helping sellers to earn money with package inserts and enabling effective and targeted marketing for advertisers.

PackVERTISE shipping partners are mostly **eBay PowerSellers & top-rated sellers**, who want to **add package inserts to their shipments**. Our partners also sell on **Amazon Marketplace**, via **online stores** or other sites.

Participation in the network is always free for sellers, the inserts will be delivered to you for free and the payout is between 1.5p-5p per insert. Coupons provided by PackVERTISE are attractive rebate coupons or samples and are **valued by buyers.**

Only the best and most reliable sellers are part of the PackVERTISE network: PackVERTISE examines every partner before approval (eg. review of shops or seller profiles; audit of shipping volume; etc.) and runs regular checks (eg. test purchases).

If you are a seller on eBay, Amazon or have an Online Store, you can earn money with package inserts for your shipments.

In addition to paid inserts, PackVERTISE offers free services for sellers, like the **DSR-Flyer for eBay,** which can help improve feedback ratings.

Find out more about PackVERTISE here: www.packvertise.co.uk

Pentagon Interactive **provides a managed service for eBay sellers who want to outsource the running of their shops.**

Founded and managed by a former powerseller and with a scalable workforce dedicated to eBay, we provide a bolt on solution for firms who just want to handle the orders in house.

If you want to grow your eBay business, you need to do the following well:

- Build and design a great looking store and listing template.
- Research your competition and categories.
- Develop an effective selling strategy.
- Set up and run automation tool software.
- Manage inventory.
- Optimize inventory.
- Provide rapid response customer service.
- React quickly and effectively to eBay platform changes.
- Develop strong relations with eBay account managers.
- Become an eBay Top Rated Seller and stay there!

We are able to help you with all of the above, and give you an eBay revenue stream which does not take away time and resources from your core business.

Our reputation within the marketplace is second to none, which is why big brands like BT and Maplin Electronics use us to manage their eBay stores.

Stuff U Sell is a hassle-free service to sell your stuff on eBay.

They are the UK's leading Trading Assistant, offering a full end-to-end selling service for both businesses and individuals looking for stress-free access to eBay. Taking care of photography and listing, storage and shipping as well as handling customer service and return, it offers a complete solution for anything from individual items to lines of excess stock and even retailers looking for an additional channel.

Stuff U Sell's excellent reputation, quality listings and experience in pricing strategies all mean higher prices; a recent survey showed upto 25% higher than market averages.

Contact - 0800 046 1100; stuffusell@stuffusell.co.uk; http://www.stuffusell.co.uk

http://www.aswas.com

Do you need help to take your eBay business forward? Are you looking to make eBay a serious sales channel? As Was have been helping their clients maximize the potential of eBay since 2001. Our personalised consulting helps sellers grow an average of 30%.

Contact us for a free consultation to assess your needs.

http://www.eauctionanorak.co.uk/

Are you baffled by eBay? Wondering if eBay can be profitable for your business? An eBay Top Rated Seller and Powerseller trading since 2002, a time served eBay trained Education Specialist providing an eBay for business consultancy service and additional virtual support via secure screen sharing remote software.

Telephone 0115 7149996 or **email** ebay@JaneBell.co.uk

NullApps - Price Spectre

http://www.pricespectre.com

Price Spectre is a dynamic pricing agent that helps sellers stay one step ahead of the competition by automatically updating their eBay and Half.com prices several times throughout the day. Users can choose between automatic and manual repricing.

Fees start as low as $2.95 per month.
Price Spectre is currently available in the eBay App Center or directly at http://www.pricespectre.com.

NullApps - Quantity Manager

http://www.qtyman.com

Scarcity sells. Quantity Manager allows sellers to improve the apparent scarcity of their fixed price listings to encourage more buying activity. When a list-ing makes a sale QM automatically refreshes the available quantity on eBay to reflect the desired amount, often in as few as six seconds. QM is currently available in the eBay App Center or directly at http://www.qtyman.com.

eBay's very own selection of seller tools for medium and large-scale sellers.

Blackthorne

http://pages.ebay.com/blackthorne/basic.html

eBay's desktop tool to create and manage listings, plus save time on buyer communication. $9.99 per month with a 30 day free trial for new users.

- Create professional-looking listings
- List in bulk, relist sold and unsold items
- Schedule listings
- Manage buyer communication

Upgrade to the Pro version for $24.99 per month, and add advanced business features:

- Inventory management
- Manage consignments and suppliers
- Bulk print shipping labels and invoices
- Monthly profit and loss reports
- Supports multiple user profiles

Listing Analytics

http://pages.ebay.com/listing_analytics/

Free application from eBay to show how your listings are performing and where they could be improved. Enable it from the *"Applications"* tab in My eBay.

- Search for a listing by keyword to see its rank in search results. Easy-to-use filtering and sorting capabilities will allow you to filter results by format, and drill down into the details of each listing to better understand your best and worst performing listings.
- View impressions, clicks and sales metrics to better understand the behaviour of your buyers. Are buyers finding your listings in search results? If so, are they clicking to view your listings? Once they click, are they buying?
- See how your listings stack up for impressions, clicks and sales against the top five results for similar Fixed Price listings.
- Get rolling 30 day trending data for impressions, clicks and sales for both active and completed listings.
- Get tips and best practices to help optimize your listings.

Selling Manager
http://pages.ebay.co.uk/selling_manager/
eBay's basic free online tool for bulk relisting and feedback, useful for busy hobby sellers:

- Save your own email templates and feedbackcomments
- Relist multiple sold and unsold listings at once
- Send feedback to multiple buyers all at once
- File, track and manage multiple unpaid items and final value fee requests

Selling Manager Pro
http://pages.ebay.co.uk/selling_manager_pro/
eBay's online tool to manage inventory and listings, and automate post-sale buyer communication. Very useful for all professional sellers. £4.99 per month, or free with

Featured/Anchor shops

- Automatically list and relist items
- Free scheduling
- Buyer auto notification; payment received, item shipped
- Auto feedback upon buyer payment/feedback
- Restock alerts Create monthly profit and loss reports
- Find out your products' success ratio and average selling price
- Download your sales history in .csv files

TurboLister
http://pages.ebay.co.uk/turbo_lister/
eBay's free desktop listing creation tool: great for all sellers whether you're a hobbyist or a busy professional with many different seller accounts.

- Add all your inventory offline, and bulk-upload when you're ready
- Synchronise with your live and ended listings for easy editing and relisting
- Easy design editor lets you create and preview professional-looking listings

File Exchange
http://pages.ebay.co.uk/file_exchange/
Free tool which enables high-volume sellers to list multiple items on eBay in a single file. Sellers can list items using flat files from an Excel spreadsheet, MS Access, or other inventory software: upload your entire inventory in one file. Perfect for uploading anexisting database:
e.g. exporting your website or your supplier's catalogue to your eBay store.

- Add, revise, re-list, and end a listing or update the status and leave feed
  back for a listing all in a single file
- Download active listings and sales history reports in a flat file format for
  importing to your own software package
- Creates the file template you need for any category, including the columns for any itemspecifics

Accounting

Managing your sales on eBay is complicated enough, but you need to manage your cash flow, profits and tax. Using an accounting tool which is integrated with eBay can make you tax returns simple as well as enabling you to product profit forecasts and manage your cash flow effectively.

Attandra T-HUB
http://www.atandra.com/ecommerce-quickbooks-integration-with-thub.html
Order Manager solution designed to integrate your Amazon, eBay, Yahoo and ecommerce stores with QuickBooks and shipping services.

Aucsys
https://www.aucsys.com/
Automated, 100% Accurate eBay Bookkeeping.

Back Office Live for eBay
http://www.mtiretail.com/
eBay and Prostores back office management.

Outright
http://outright.com/
Automatically record and organize all your income and expenses from PayPal, bank and credit cards and import scanned-in receipts and cash expenditures.

SageFire KeepMore.net
https://www.keepmore.net/?page=ebay
Automatically import all of your eBay transactions every hour and allocates them as income or expense for you.

Teapplix
http://www.teapplix.com/how/quickbooks.html
eBay, PayPal, Amazon, Buy.com, ShoppingCart Order Download to QuickBooks.

Tradebox
http://www.tradebox.uk.com/
Automated bookkeeping tool, downloading orders from eBay, Amazon, Play.com, ChannelAdvisor, Magento, Shopcreator, EKM Powershop and LiquidShop and creating all of the financial entries required in Sage to account for your online sales.

TransManager for PayPal
http://www.pp-manager.com/
Manage your PayPal transactions directly from my eBay. Automatically match eBay and PayPal transactions, compare paid amounts and postal codes from one place.

Zed Systems

Products designed to make getting information in or out of QuickBooks as easy as possible.

If you use an Apple Mac you're probably frustrated that many eBay tools are built for windows only. These are the premier products designed just for you and guaranteed to work on you Apple computer.

Auction Tender
http://www.colourfull.com/at40.html
Inventory and Customer Management with templates for both auctions or ecommerce web sites for Apple Macs.

AuctionGenie
http://auctiongenie.luxcentral.com/
Apple Mac solution to manage selling, buying, tracking, and related activities for eBay.com.

eLister
http://blackmagik.com/elister.html
Apple Mac eBay auction utility which lets you create your auction listings offline, at your own convenience.

Garage Sale
http://www.iwascoding.com/garagesale/
Apple Mac full-featured client application for eBay edit to enable you to track and manage all your auctions with one single application.

iSale
http://www.equinux.com/us/products/isale/index.html
A simple, easy to use app for eBay to create compelling layouts and professional designs in a drag and drop interface.

There are eBay tools in My eBay, TurboLister, Selling Manager and File Exchange which can help you bulk edit your eBay listings, but these specialized tools make the job quick and simple and can edit anything from 1 to 100s of listings in one operation.

Comsulting Bulk Reviser
http://www.comsulting-limited.com/software/store/
Bulk revise / edit all aspects of your eBay listings with the Comsulting Bulk Reviser Windows desktop application.

Froo! Bulk Revision eBay App
http://www.froo.com/bulk_revision/?ref
Find & Replace Titles, Description, Returns Policies, Start Price, Buy it Now Price, Reserve Price, Add/Remove Quantity, Modify Handling Time, Alter PayPal Address and Item Condition.

eBay isn't just about selling, if you want to buy smart there are a range of tools available varying from finding items which have been mis-spelt and so have few bids to sniping tools to enable you to place your bid at the very last minute.

AuctionGenie
http://auctiongenie.luxcentral.com/
Apple Mac solution to manage selling, buying, tracking, and related activities for eBay.com.

AuctionTamer
http://www.auctiontamer.com
AuctionTamer is a customized tabbed Internet browser with a built-in auction item watch list for international eBay sites.

Auction Sniper
http://www.auctionsniper.com
eBay sniper that automates the process of placing your eBay bid in the closing seconds of an auction.

AuctionTrax
http://auctiontrax.com/
A free service to track, search, watch and bid on one or more eBay auctions - with just a few clicks.

Fatfingers
http://www.fatfingers.co.uk/
Find mis-spelt items on eBay.

nabit
http://us.nabit.com/index.jsp
Bid from your desktop with pop-up notifications if you've been outbid, if you've won or lost, if the price changes on an item you're watching, or if your auction is about to expire.

SearchDome
http://www.searchdome.com/
Free eBay automation search tool for active eBay buyers.

Looking for support to take your eBay business to the next level? Seek the advice of a specialist.

As Was
http://www.aswas.com
As Was have been helping their clients maximize the potential of eBay since 2001.

Jane Bell - eBay Specialist Consultant
http://www.eauctionanorak.co.uk/
A time served eBay trained Education Specialist providing an eBay for business consultancy service and additional virtual support via secure screen sharing remote software.

Don't just sell one product to your customers; sell multiple products with cross merchandising. Make sure that your buyers know what else you have to offer and give them incentives and discounts to buy from you again.

eTextAlert
http://www.etextalert.com/
Put an alert sign-up form directly in your auction listing to give potential buyers an easy way to get a last minute reminder about an eBay auction item they may want to bid on.

MyStoreMaps
http://www.mystoremaps.com/
Boost buyer confidence while building seller credibility with a fun and useful tool for their shopping experience. Get a MyStoreMap in all your auction, BIN, and store style listings to show where in the world previous buyers live.

MyStoreRewards
http://www.mystorerewards.com
Offer your own, turn-key, reward program. As long as you accept PayPal payments, in just 10 minutes, any seller selling anything, anywhere in the world, can use MyStoreRewards to drive repeat sales and grow profits.

Review Gadget
http://applications.ebay.com/selling?ViewEAppDetails&appType=1&appId=review.merchantgadgets.com
Review Gadget collects detailed product reviews and displays them on your listing pages.

Wiqet photo, voice slides
http://applications.ebay.com/selling?ViewEAppDetails&stab=3&appType=1&appId=photo.wiqet.com
Create a photo slideshow, with the option to add your personal voice message or a music file, and add it to your 'selling items'.

ZippyQuiz
http://zippyquiz.com
A free tool that allows any eBay sell to display their listings and other eBay information on their website, blog and any site where they can include a small code snippet.

SellerFox
http://www.sellerfox.com/homepage.html?L=1
Range of powerful slideshow galleries for your eBay auctions.

Auction Nudge
http://www.auctionnudge.com
A free tool that allows any eBay sell to display their listings and other eBay information on their website, blog and any site where they can include a small code snippet.

AuctionFB
http://www.auctionfb.com/
Free tool to enable you to display your eBay feedback on your own website.

slideLynxx
http://www.auctionlynxx.com/
Automatically embed a marketing module which dynamically categorizes your items to improve the merchandising experience for your buyers.

BayURL
http://bayurl.com
Transforms long, complicated eBay links into small ones.

BidVertiser
http://www.bidvertiser.com/
Drive buyers and increase sales by placing an automatically created ad for any of your eBay Items on thousands of relevant websites.

Sales in a Click
http://salesinaclick.com/?edition=ebay
Drive sales with engaging relevant and professionally produced and written email marketing.

Auctionpixie
http://www.auctionpixie.co.uk/
Cross-promote your items using a choice of free scrolling galleries.

PayCodes
http://www.paycodes.com/
PayCodes enables merchants to create specific coupon codes that can be given to customers and used towards future PayPal payments.

scrolleo
http://scrolleo.com/
Create a complete scrolling gallery with just your eBay username. You can use your code immediately in your auctions and change the design of your scrolleo any time without having to revise any of your eBay auctions.

Ayee Gallery
http://www.ayee.net
Present your complete eBay listings with the cross-promotional tool Ayee Gallery Unlimited.

edeetion

http://www.edeetion.com/

Use your web pages to promote your auctions, and increase your sells on eBay with an eBay seller widget - a small but efficient web application permanently connected to your eBay seller account.

You can have the best product in the world at the lowest possible price, but just retail shops spend hours arranging goods to look as attractive as possible these suppliers can help you design your eBay shop and eBay listings to give a professional image. Design isn't just about looking good though, with a quality shop and listing design you'll find your sales increase as buyers are tempted to browse through your products and most design include an array of tools to promote similar items and your top selling products.

As Was
http://www.aswas.com
Founded in 1995, As Was offers full-service and completely custom website design and installation. We take a marketing firm's approach, so every design is from scratch, and created for your company's personality and image. Our experience includes Wordpress, Volusion, Magento, ChannelAdvisor Stores, Zen-Cart, Vendio Stores, and many more.

Contact us today for a free consultation.
Advansys
http://www.ebay-store-design.co.uk
Bring a professional look to your ebay shop & listings with eBay Store design listing tools and cross channel ecommerce.

ebayshopdesign
http://www.ebayshopdesign.com/
eBay shop design, listing design, about me page design, custom page design and logo design.

Ebeezy
http://www.ebeezy.com
Custom eBay store adn template design to allow you to make the most out of your eBay business.

esellersolutions
http://www.esellersolutions.com/
Professionally designed eBay shop and item template design with full ecommerce enabled website populated with your products from eBay.

Frooition
http://www.frooition.com/
Advanced eBay design - Professional design for your eBay store & listings with powerful functionality to boost your eBay sales.

Just Template IT
http://www.justtemplateit.co.uk/
Full solution eBay Advanced store design from logo design to a branded eBay store.

kooki web design
http://www.kookiweb.co.uk
Specialist eBay shop design, e-Commerce and website packages at prices you can afford.

LaunchPad Auctions
http://www.launchpadauctions.com/
Custom eBay Store Design and Auctions Design, including templates, flash, and logo design.

Sell It Smart
http://sell-it-smart.co.uk/
Custom-tailored eBay store and listing design along with websites, business cards, flyers and other print media.

Seller Source Book
http://www.sellersourcebook.com/
3000+ Auction Templates for eBay.com & UK with Multi-Quantity Variations and free scheduling. Compatible with TurboLister.

Store Design Themes
http://applications.ebay.com/selling?ViewEAppDetails&stab=1&appType=1&appId=store.mypmit.com
Custom animated professional appearance to your eBay store for eBay.com.

VaroLogic
http://www.varologic.com/
Webstore and eBay design and management with universal template to create uniform listings.

PageMage
http://pagemage.com/
Free eBay templates, listing software and social sharing tools with video, moving text and
slideshows.

Tempino Templates
http://www.tempino.com/index.php?p=products&view=ebay_templates
Hundreds of eBay templates, auction templates, and designer themes to make your listings
stand out.

Auction Designs
http://www.auction-designs.com/services.htm
eBay store and template and ecommerce design and marketing solutions.

Auction Zealot
http://www.auctionzealot.com/
Easy listings with supersize images, captions and free scheduling.

Dzine-hub
http://www.dzine-hub.com
Consistent branding with a custom eBay store design & listing template design with creative cross-selling & cross-promotion.

If you're running out of warehouse space or simply don't have the time and resources to ship your products then outsourcing your fulfillment is the solution. These companies specialize in holding your stock and picking, packing and shipping it to your customers leaving you free to concentrate on selling.

Webgistix GlobalFill
http://www.webgistix.com/
Never again have to pack another box, order materials, count inventory, hire labour, file paperwork, handle returns, look for space, or worry about growing your order fulfilment operations to meet demand.

eFulfillment Service
http://www.efulfillmentservice.com/ebay-fulfillment/
eFulfillment Service including receiving, product inspection, storage, order fulfillment, shipping, and returns processing.

Royal Mail Warehousing and Distribution
http://www.royalmail.com/portal/rm/jump2?catId=500029&mediaId=500032
Warehouse and Distribution solution providing integrated eCommerce, stock management and order fulfilment service that drives growth and great customer service with complete control.

Shipwire
http://www.shipwire.com/
Outsource some or all of your warehousing and shipping storage, the packing, the shipping and other logistical details are handled by Shipwire from all your ecommerce sites.

Tools for rapid deployment and growth. There comes a time when managing a multichannel retail business across eBay and other online marketplaces and webstores becomes too labour intensive to be commecially viable. Management tools allow sellers to handle large volumes of listings and sales by automating many processes and allowing you to concentrate on building profits.

247 TopSeller
http://www.247topseller.co.uk/
MultiChannel ecommerce solution for eBay, Amazon, Play, Pixmania and webstore.

4SELLERS
http://www.4sellers.de/
Complete inventory, accounting and logistics with multi-channel distribution through marketplaces such as eBay, Amazon or Yatego.

AdLister
http://www.ad-lister.co.uk
An advanced content management tool that controls an eBay store or your website.

Afterbuy
http://www.afterbuy.de/
MultiChannel marketing, logistics, payment, communication and webstore solution.

AppEagle Inventory
http://www.appeagle.com/
Manage inventory, create schedules and set dynamic pricing across multiple selling platforms such as eBay, Amazon and Buy.com.

Auction Sound
http://www.auctionsound.com/
Complete eBay Auction Management Software with eBay consignment and online inventory management.

Auction Tender
http://www.colourfull.com/at40.html
Inventory and Customer Management with templates for both auctions or ecommerce web sites for Apple Macs.

Auction Wizard
http://www.auctionwizard2000.com/
Complete auction management solution for eBay, eBay Stores and Overstock.com Auctions.

AuctionBlox
http://www.auctionblox.com
Easily advertise your products on eBay, Google and your own online store all from a centralised dashboard.

AuctionGenie
http://auctiongenie.luxcentral.com/
Apple Mac solution to manage selling, buying, tracking, and related activities for eBay.com.

AuctionSage
http://www.auctionsagesoftware.com/
Desktop software to manage eBay, Amazon, Overstock.com and Bidville.com.

AuctionSplash
http://www.auctionsplash.com/
Desktop eBay tools designed to make it easier for you to buy and sell on eBay.

Auctiva
http://www.auctiva.com/
Your Complete Solution for Selling on eBay. Try it all for FREE!

BayLister
http://raewycksoftware.com/
A desktop application designed to provide an easy and quick way to create and post auction listings on eBay.

Cascade
http://www.cascade-uk.com/
Ecommerce Website that integrates all of your online sales from eBay, Amazon, Priceminister and Play.

CDC Ecommerce (Formerly Truition)
http://www.truition.com/
Advanced and comprehensive eCommerce technology as an on-demand service.

Channel Velocity
http://www.channelvelocity.com
MultiChannel Management solutions to improve inventory yield.

ChannelAdvisor
http://channeladvisor.com
MultiChannel Management for Marketplaces, Paid Search, Comparison Shopping, Webstore and Rich Media.

ChannelMAX
http://www.channelmax.net/
Manage Centrally, Sell Globally on eBay, Amazon, Buy.COM and PriceGrabber.

ChannelVelocity OnRamp
http://www.channelvelocity.com
MultiChannel retailing suited for sellers with large product catalogs, multiple users, and high volume warehouse operations.

CORESense LaunchPad for eBay
http://www.coresense.com/products/sbebay/index.html
Component of CORESense's Integrated Retail Management - everything you need to easily and successfully do business on eBay.

eDock
http://www.edock.it/Default.aspx
eDock applications that allow you to manage inventory and orders coming from your eCommerce site or eBay.

eLister
http://blackmagik.com/elister.html
Apple Mac eBay auction utility which lets you create your auction listings of-fline, at your own convenience.

eseller Pro
http://www.esellerpro.com/
eSellerPro is a complete MultiChannel business management system that integrates the whole online sales process, simplifying and automating tasks such as inventory management, product listing and scheduling, sales order processing, payment and dispatch, customer communications and accounts posting.

eSelling Tools
http://www.esellingtools.com
Complete solution for selling on eBay.

Garage Sale
http://www.iwascoding.com/garagesale/
Apple Mac full-featured client application for eBay edit to enable you to track and manage all your auctions with one single application.

imOnline
http://www.imonlinegroup.com/
An ecommerce package consisting of a wide range of ecommerce services for different kinds of clients.

Infopia
http://www.infopia.com/
eCommerce solution to manage inventory across multiple online channels and creating enterprise level websites.

inkFrog
http://www.inkfrog.com/
Everything you need to launch and manage eBay listings and sell more efficiently and effectively.

iSale
http://www.equinux.com/us/products/isale/index.html
A simple, easy to use app for eBay to create compelling layouts and professional designs in a drag and drop interface.

Kyozou
http://www.kyozou.com/
MultiChannel web-based software with everything you need to manage and run your online business.

Linnworks
http://www.linnworks.com/
MultiChannel eBay, Amazon, Play, Pixmania and Webstore order management and inventory control.

Listomax
http://www.listomax.com/
eBay listing software that makes it simple to list your items.

Luna
http://www.dikoro.com
Luna will gather information held in the Sage 50 database and submit this to eBay and allow you to save your eBay product description and format to Sage 50.

Make-A-Store
http://www.make-a-store.com
Shopping cart solution starts with all the features and functionality of the eBay with the powerful Divinity E-commerce platform.

Mercent Retail
http://www.mercent.com/solutions_marketplace.aspx
Mercent Retail Marketplace helps online retailers promote their products across online transactional marketplaces like Amazon and eBay.

Merchant Run
http://www.merchantrun.com/
Complete auction management solutions and expertise that revolutionize the way eBay multi-site business is conducted.

Monsoon
http://www.monsoonworks.com
MultiChannel media solution for eBay, Amazon, Able Books, Alibris, half.com,

Play, Blackwell, Barnes & Noble and Borders.

One Stop Order Processing
http://www.1stoporders.com/
Order processing to manage orders from Ebay, Amazon, RomanCart, Actinic, Playtrade, eBid, osCommerce, mail order and telephone orders in the same place.

PayPal Batch Printing
http://paypalbatchprinting.codegoose.com/
Print multiple invoices, shipping labels or packing slips in one go.

Pentagon Interactive
http://www.pentagon-interactive.co.uk/
Pentagon can directly managing your eBay shops or add value to areas where you do not have the time, resources, or knowledge to realise the full sales potential of your products.

Plenty Markets
http://www.plentymarkets.de/
MultiChannel solution for eBay, Amazon, Ricardo, Auvito, Gimahhot, Tradoria, Mercateo, Yatego and PIXmania.

Quantity Manager
http://www.qtyman.com
Quantity Manager allows sellers to improve the apparent scarcity of their fixed price listings to encourage more buying activity.

Sales Harvester
http://www.salesharvester.com
Advanced MultiChannel inventory management software designed to integrate with all eBay, Amazon and OSCommerce sites.

Selro
http://www.selro.com/
MultiChannel Selling Platform eBay, Amazon, Google Base and your own ecommerce site from a centralised inventory.

SixBit
http://www.sixbitsoftware.com
Intuitive, flexible software that can grow with you as you build your ecommerce business.

Stone Edge Order Manager
http://www.stoneedge.com/main/order-manager/
Order Manager with quick and easy integration from multiple shopping carts and sales channels.

Supreme Auction

http://www.supreme-auction.com/ http://www.supreme-auction.de/

eBay listing tool, template designs and cross marketing widgets for eBay.com Germany and UK.

Teapplix

http://www.teapplix.com/how.html

MultiChannel webservice technology to automatically download new orders and update shipping status from eBay, Amazon, buy.com, Yahoo, half.com and PayPal.

Total Auction Management

http://www.totalauctionmanagement.com/

Manage your auctions and eliminate up to ninety percent of manual processes.

Ultimate Feed

http://www.ultimatefeed.com/

Build a data feed for MultiChannels including eBay, Amazon, NextTAG, Shopzilla, Google, and TradeDoubler.

Powa

http://powa.com

Quickly and easily create a professional website and push your product catalogue to affiliates like, Google Base, PayPal offers and eBay.

Vendio

http://www.vendio.com/

MultiChannel solution - Create your items once and sell through multiple marketplaces including eBay, Amazon and Webstore.

Zazanaire

http://www.ubeha.com/

Manage transactions and activities at client side instead of login to eBay.com.

Zoovy

https://www.zoovy.com

MultiChannel management for Amazon, Buy.com & eBay with real-time inventory tracking.

M2E Pro eBay Magento Integration

http://m2epro.ess-ua.com/

Integrate Magento and eBay to quickly and easily create and manage listings, synchronize stock level and import eBay transactions and orders.

Solid Commerce

http://www.solidcommerce.com/Index.htm

MultiChannel eCommerce platform with centralize inventory for eBay, Amazon, half.com.

eBay SuperStore CRM
http://www.softwareprojects.com/ebay-superstore-crm.php
All-inclusive Selling Solution, designed to streamline every aspect of your eBay Business.

Fillz Sales Management
http://www.fillz.com
MultiChannel solution to enable you to load your inventory once and list on more than 20 different fixed-price marketplaces.

AuctionLinc
http://www.auctionlinc.com/
Over 200+ HTML Templates, easy to use Lister and Image Uploader, auto relisting, slide shows and scheduling.

Auction Scheduler
http://www.auctionscheduler.com/
Professional web-based scheduling for your eBay listings.

AuctionSound
http://www.auctionsound.com/
Complete Craigslist and eBay Listing Management Software.

My Photo Partner Auction Manager
http://mpp.myphotos.cc/amsignup1.asp?cs=P250&
Web-Based auction manager with Inventory control, one page listing form, unlimited photos with captions, scheduled listing and automated relisting of unsold items and relaunch of identical items after a sale.

SalesX
http://salesx.irusgroup.com/salesx/index.aspx
End to end solution that provides complete business management and control over the sales process on eBay.com.

Auction Street
http://www.auction-street.com/
Inventory management for your eBay Business.

Sellernet
http://www.sellernet.co.uk/
Power multiple retail channels with comprehensive Warehouse Management and Order Fulfillment functionality for mail-order/ e-commerce operations.

SellerExpress
http://www.sellerexpress.com/
SellerExpress is a complete package for managing every step of the market-place sales cycle including inventory management, auto price checking, order fulfillment, customer emails, shipping, currency conversion and much more.

ChannelGrapper
http://www.ChannelGrabber.com
MultiChannel solution combining your eBay and Amazon accounts inventory with all your orders from eBay and Amazon managed in one combined system.

Aerolister Pro
http://www.aerolister.com/
eBay compatible automatic relisting, selling and feedback sending application.

Price Spectre
http://www.pricespectre.com
Price Spectre is a dynamic pricing agent that helps sellers stay one step ahead of the competition by automatically updating their eBay and Half.com prices several times throughout the day.

With mobile tools you can buy and sell directly from your mobile phone. Whether you want tools to manage your business or simply to scan a barcode from a CD using your iPhone and list it for sale on eBay in seconds these are the must have apps for your mobile cell phone.

iRibbit
http://www.iribbit.com/
Search, watch, bid and selling tool for mobile cell phones.

Mobile Auction Manager
http://www.mobileauctionmanager.co.uk/
Keep a close track of your eBay Auctions on the move by allowing you to view your current
auctions as well as getting alerts when you've been outbid or a watched item is ending soon.

Alterme iPhone Power Seller Tools
http://itunes.apple.com/us/app/ebay-seller-tools/id343505826?mt=8
List an item with the pictures from iPhone Camera or Photo Album, relist the item with one tap and leave bulk feedback on eBay.

Garage Sale
http://www.iwascoding.com/garagesale/
GarageSale touch and GarageSale HD offer all the features you need to get your stuff onto eBay while you are on the road with your iPhone, your iPod touch or your iPad.

eBay on iPhone
http://ebay.co.uk/mobile/iphone.html
eBay iPhone app.

eBay on iPad
http://ebay.co.uk/mobile/ipad.html
eBay iPad app.

eBay on Android
http://ebay.co.uk/mobile/android.html
eBay Android app.

eBay on Blackberry
http://ebay.co.uk/mobile/blackberry.html
eBay Blackberry app.

eBay on Window 7 Mobile
http://ebay.co.uk/mobile/windows-phone.html
eBay Windows 7 Mobile app.

Do you want to know when someone leaves you a low feedback DSR? Do you want a text message when your item sells on eBay? How about a Windows gadget to monitor your eBay activity direct from your Windows desktop? These tools will keep you in touch with what's happening on eBay.

ah!TEXT
http://applications.ebay.com/selling?ViewEAppDetails&appType=1&appId=ahtxtapp.ahtxt.com
Get SMS text messages when you receive bids, sales, best offers, questions, feedback and disputes.

AuctionMonitor
http://www.auctionmonitor.net/
Widgets and gadgets that can help you put your My eBay information in more convenient places, direct access to the status of auctions listed on eBay from the comfort of your desktop.

BayToGo
http://www.baytogo.com/
Stay connected with your sales/auctions on eBay by text message, whether you are on the road, travelling abroad, in the office or simply roaming around.

DSR Watch
http://dsrwatch.com/
Get a Detailed Seller Rating report by entering an eBay seller's user ID.

ESR Auction Watcher
http://www.cr1spy.co.uk/ESR/Default.aspx
A desktop application to help you search for and keep track of eBay auctions whether you are a seller or a buyer.

Visitra
http://www.visitra.com/
Find WHO, WHEN and from WHERE comes to your eBay auctions and improve your marketing strategy.

DSR Report
http://www.dsrreport.com/
Detailed free DSR report to show which items provide the best DSR scores, how many of your buyers left you 1's or 2's and a breakdown by country.

Communicating with your eBay buyers efficiently can increase your sales. A CRM (Customer Relationship Management) tool can streamline questions and answers to your customers and effective post-sales marketing can bring back previous buyers and turn them into repeat customers.

Auction Contact
http://www.auctioncontact.net/
Increase auction sales by attracting new customers and increasing customer loyalty by constantly letting them know about your merchandise and auctions.

AuctionThanx
http://auctionthanx.com/
Build your eBay Buyer Relationship from their very first win. Start building that relationship right now, automatically send a customised email to every auction winner.

Canvasee FREE Advertising
http://applications.ebay.com/selling?ViewEAppDetails&stab=1&mId=2000020&appType=1&appId=Stileit
Promote and advertise your listings online through social media including blogs and social networks like Facebook and other web pages by enabling your customers to share their findings with others.

ezSupport
https://www.hostedsupport.com
Integrated with eBay's *"Ask a question"* form, ezSupport for eBay is designed to eliminate the many repetitive questions received by eBay sellers.

fflap
http://www.fflap.com/
A marketing and advertising platform to help eBay sellers get more profit for their eBay listings using social networks like Twitter and Facebook.

ReplyManager
http://www.replymanager.com/
Web-based email management tool created to help eBay Marketplace sellers manage high volume incoming email by integrating directly to eBay's API and automatically organizing email into Topic Folders.

Cloud Conversion eCommSource
http://cloudconversion.com/solutions
eCommerce platform independent, Customer Relationship Management (CRM) solution available to eBay sellers to manage all customer service and support operations from a single source and entirely within salesforce.com's Service Cloud 2.

Whilst many eBay buyers are happy to use eBay's PayPal these are the approved payment methods you can use to accept payments on eBay. Use your own credit card merchant processing account and make sure if you're selling on International Sites in countries where PayPal isn't a de facto standard that you can accept payments in the currencies and methods which buyers habitually use.

Allpay.net
http://www.allpay.net

Bill Me Later
http://www.billmelater.com/

CertaPay
http://www.certapay.com

Checkfree.com
http://www.checkfree.com

hyperwallet.com
http://www.hyperwallet.com

Moneybookers.com
http://www.moneybookers.com

Nochex.com
http://www.nochex.com

Ozpay.biz
http://www.ozpay.biz

Paymate.com.au
http://www.paymate.com.au

PayPal
http://www.paypal.com

Propay.com
http://www.propay.com

XOOM
http://www.xoom.com

Auctionchex
http://www.auctionchex.com

eBay enables you to display pictures in your eBay listings, but with these tools you can crop, clean and manipulate images, host multiple images at no additional costs, create galleries and slide shows and ensure your customers can see exactly what you have to sell.

123Show
http://www.123show.com
Show more sell more with zoom, rotation, colour change, hotspots and multiple views.

AAA Seller
http://www.aaaseller.com
Simple Drag-and-Drop picture upload utility with rotate and arrange your images automatically created thumbnails from your uploaded pics and super-zoom technology.

AuctionPix
http://www.auctionpix.co.uk/
Image Hosting for your eBay auctions, upload up to 5 images at a time, manage your images, you can delete any unwanted images at any time and create folders to organise your images.

irisize
http://www.irisize.com/
Build your own banners, images and webpages.

Village Photos
http://www.villagephotos.com/
Free or paid image hosting optimised for eBay sellers.

My Auction Gallery
http://mygallery.timegonebuy.com/index.html
My Auction Gallery provides powerful image hosting capabilities. Use MAGPICs studio to modify, enhance and watermark your images.

Blingit
http://www.vertustech.com/blingit/
Transform ordinary product shots into extraordinary ones unbelievably quickly and easily. Designed for everyone from the novice user to businessman and web designer.

Fluid Mask
http://www.vertustech.com/fluidMask/overview.html
The #1 Still-Image Masking Tool Photoshop cut-out plug-in to separate your product shot from the background.

There are three main sources of products for eBay sellers, other than sourcing direct from the manufacturer. You can source excess, end of line or refurbished products, choose a drop shipper who will hold stock and ship on your behalf, or source a supplier who will manufacture products to your exact specification.

Alibaba
http://www.alibaba.com/
The source for finding suppliers and manufacturers.

Doba
http://www.doba.com/
Access to millions of wholesale products, drop-shipped directly to your customers.

Drop Ship Business
http://www.dropship-business.com
Access to over one million wholesale and dropship products all in one place.

Salehoo
http://www.salehoo.com/
Dropshippers, manufacturers, wholesalers and liquidators for every type of product imaginable.

Shopster
http://www.shopster.com/
Network for dropship suppliers and sellers to connect.

Stockshifters
http://stockshifters.com/
Trade marketplace for surplus, clearance and returned stock.

Worldwide Brands
http://www.worldwidebrands.com/
Wholesale Dropshipping And Drop Ship Directory.

The Wholesaler
http://www.thewholesaler.co.uk
Wholesale Trade Directory.

Bitsy
http://bitsythis.com/
Find people to help your business grow and let other businesses find you too.

The Wholesale Forums
http://www.thewholesaleforums.co.uk/
UK's leading B2B community and marketplace for wholesalers, importers, dropshippers, retailers and trade buyers.

Research

These are the tools and services which can really save you money. Discover what the hot selling products on eBay are, find the products which are selling at the best prices and if you're selling find out how much your stock will be worth before you go ahead and purchase it. Smart eBay sellers make their profits when buying their stock as they know exactly what price it will fetch when they sell it.

Auction Inspector
http://www.auctioninspector.com/
Inspects posts on the eBay *"want it now"* section and tells you which products are wanted most often.

AuctionIntelligence
http://www.certes.net/AuctionIntelligence/Server/features.aspx
Search through millions of eBay listings to find the top selling items that match your search on eBay.com, UK and Australia.

AuctionYen
http://www.auctionyen.com/
Uncover hidden product and niche ideas from eBay's want it now section.

eBay Research Labs BayEstimator
http://labs.ebay.com/erl/demoto/to
Optimise Your eBay Listing Title's BayEstimate to find the best keywords for your product.

Get4It
http://www.get4it.co.uk/
Find the best deals possible on eBay and eBay Motors by category or search by keyword.

Goofbay
http://www.goofbay.com/
eBay sniper, not in title search, mis-spelt search, seller history, seller feedback, best offers and eBay most popular search tools.

Hammertap
http://www.hammertap.com/
eBay research tool to discover what products to sell and how to make more sales more often.

iTaggit
http://www.itaggit.com/
Research prices before you buy or sell antiques and collectibles vintage to modern.

Mr.Research
http://www.mrresearch.com/
Analyse your competition and view Top and Flop Items for every Seller and Category with 2 years category trends.

priceLista
http://www.pricelista.net/
Identify the correct price at which to sell products on eBay, buyers and sellers can create item searches that can be run repeatedly.

PriceMiner
http://www.priceminer.com
Your online price guide for art, antiques & collectibles with more than 27million prices from realised prices from eBay, GoAntiques and TIAS.

Sellebrity Analytics
http://sellebrity.com/
eBay analytics made easy - use your past data to make future decisions.

Sellerwise
http://www.sellerwise.net/
Real time eBay analytics to reveal the search terms customers used to find your listing.

Terapeak
https://www.terapeak.com
Stay ahead of your competition. See the products your competitors are making the most money with. Track their total sales, average prices, listing strategies, and more.

Toolhaus
http://toolhaus.org/
Reasearch your own or someone else's eBay feedback and check your blocked bidder list for NARU buyers.

WatchCount
http://www.watchcount.com
What's Most Popular on eBay, as Voted by eBay Users who have added the item to their watched list.

eBay.com Popular Products
http://product-index.ebay.com/best_selling_1.html
The most popular products on eBay.com.

eBay.co.uk Popular Products
http://product-index.ebay.co.uk/best_selling_1.html
The most popular products on eBay.co.uk.

Watched Item

http://www.watcheditem.com/

Watched Item finds the most interesting and most watched auctions on eBay.

Terapeak for PayPal

http://www.analytics.terapeak.com/

Manage your online business with fact-based decisions- Terapeak for PayPal provides you these facts in a time saving and visual toolset and learn where to save money with simple reports that show you where your money goes.

Sellathon

http://www.sellathon.com/

Powerful, easy-to-use analytics you can use to optimize your listings.

Returns are a byproduct of online selling and all good sellers will offer a refund or exchange service. Streamline your returns processes by making it easy for your customers to return products and have an audit trail so that you know exactly what's been returned and who needs refunding.

PhiConnect Return Service
http://applications.ebay.com/selling?ViewEAppDetails&stab=1&mId=200002
0&appType=1&appId=returntool.phiconnect.com
Accept and manage return requests and inquiries online with streamlined returns and integrated customer communications.

ReturnEasy
http://returneasy.com
Provide a professional RMA system to sellers and customers registration process is very with automatic linking to your eBay account.

Shipping is something every eBay seller has to do and these tools can make that easier for you. These tools can produce invoices with integrated labels at the click of a mouse, can produce shipping labels for your chosen courier, or can source a one off delivery for that oversized over weight item that needs a specialist carrier to deliver.

TShip
http://applications.ebay.com/selling?ViewEAppDetails&stab=3&appType=1&appId=smapp.teapplix.com
Generate up to 2000 labels in one batch. Quickly print out shipping labels from saved product information including weight, dimensions and shipping options.

AdShip Express
http://www.adshipexpress.com
Get a discount or rewards points for including an advertisement in each package that you ship.

Auctane Shipping Manager
http://www.auctane.net/Default.aspx
Batch print multiple shipping labels with just a few clicks with payment of USPS postage via Stamps.com.

Deliveryquotecompare
http://www.deliveryquotecompare.com/
Save time and money by comparing quotes from 100's of registered transport companies.

Priory Direct Integrated Labels
http://www.priorydirect.co.uk/
Your source for integrated shipping labels, packaging, laser labels, paper and toner cartridges.

Endicia
http://www.endicia.com/
Print internet postage for mail and packages online from your PC or MAC.

GetItNext SM
http://sm.getitnext.com/
For domestic US eBay freight and coming soon, international eBay shipping, Save by receiving a freight discount usually only available to volume shippers.

Just Ship IT
http://www.justshipit.co.uk/
Invoice and labelling software with eBay and Amazon integration to produce invoices and labels with Royal Mail PPI Integration.

Link to UPS WorldShip

http://applications.ebay.com/selling?ViewEAppDetails&stab=1&mId=200002
0&appType=1&appId=com.ebay.ups.worldship

Link to UPS WorldShip can help you reduce the time and effort it takes to process your eBay shipments.

MyHermes

https://www.myhermes.co.uk

Simple, convenient and the cheapest 3-5 day door to door delivery service in the UK integrated with eBay and pay with PayPal.

OrderCup Shipping

http://www.ordercup.com/

Streamline and automate order management and tracking for with real-time, precise order status from the point of ordering to delivery.

Packing Partner

http://www.aimcosoftware.co.uk/packingpartner.html

Collects data from eBay, Amazon, and websites and format addresses, print labels, picking and packing lists and VAT or non-VAT invoices.

PackVERTISE

http://www.packvertise.co.uk/

Connecting advertisers and online retailers, enabling effective marketing and helping sellers to earn money with package advertisement inserts.

Papilion

http://www.superizzi.com/papilion/

Download transactions from eBay, send updates back to eBay, print invoices & labels, generate picking list and track orders to delivery.

Parcel2Go

http://www.parcel2go.com/

Global courier company offering cheap shipping services across the UK and internationally with some of the world's largest couriers including DHL, FedEx and Parcelforce.

PayPerParcel

http://www.payperparcel.co.uk/

Great discounts off the normal selling rates from DHL, send from as little as just one Parcel
Shiply.

http://www.shiply.com

find cheap courier services UK by matching yourself up with UK couriers & delivery service companies already making similar trips across Europe. Courier companies bid for your business.

ShipRush
http://my.shiprush.com/
Unify your shipping To Do list in one place from ecommerce sites like eBay, Amazon and PayPal as well as carts like ZenCart, Magento and others.

ShipSaver Insurance
http://www.shipsaver.biz/
Offers eBay Selling Manager users savings over USPS, add insurance to items in bulk with a few mouse clicks and file claims online.

Shipwire
http://www.shipwire.com
Outsource some or all of your warehousing and shipping storage, the packing, the shipping and other logistical details are handled by Shipwire from all your ecommerce sites.

Shipworks
http://www.interapptive.com/
Downloads your order and create shipping labels, manage customers and emails, and update the online status of each order.

Stamps.com
http://stamps.com
Print U.S. postage from your PC, receive discounts you can't get at the Post Office and import orders from eBay, Amazon.com and more.

uship
http://www.uship.com/ebay/shippingcenter.aspx
Simultaneously manage your eBay and uShip activities all in one place with accurate delivery estimates and an easy way to transport your auction items.

Metapack
http://www.metapack.com/
Order from anywhere, despatch from anywhere, deliver to anywhere and monitor the delivery whilst in transit from anywhere, MetaPack software works with all parcel carriers and manages the entire home delivery process.

ParcelMonkey
http://www.parcelmonkey.co.uk/
Low cost door-to-door UK and International parcel delivery delivery service.

Smart Courier
http://www.smartcourier.co.uk/
Parcel delivery service for the one off and occasional shippers to businesses in all industries which is fully trackable.

If you want to manage your trading assistant business then there's software to help you manage the consignments your customers bring in and track sales and profits plus payments due to customers. If you're looking for a trading assistant to help you sell then this is the place to start.

Liberty4 Trading Assistants
http://resaleworld.com/products.php?group=2
e-consignment software designed to meet the demanding needs of drop-off and econsignment
businesses.

AuctionWagon
http://www.auctionwagon.com/
Drop off store management software to increase productivity and simplify management.

Meridian
http://www.noblespirit.com/
Consignment tracking fully integrated with online automated auction listing and management.

Stuff U Sell
http://www.stuffusell.co.uk
UK's leading Trading Assistant offering a full end-to-end hassle-free service selling service for both businesses and individuals.

eBay UK Directory
http://pages.ebay.co.uk/tradingassistants/hire-trading-assistant.html
eBay UK Trading Assistant directory searchable by location.

eBay.com Directory
http://ebaytradingassistant.com/directory/index.php?page=home
eBay.com Trading Assistant Directory searchable by location.

eBay is a worldwide platform and if you want to sell into eBay countries where there's a language difference then having your listings translated into the local language will increase sales. These professional translation companies specialize in translating eBay listings for international sellers.

InterCultural Elements
http://www.intercultural-elements.eu/
Translators who incorporate cultural specifics and knowledge of e-commerce to ensure your ads are both appealing and technically accurate.

Webinterpret
http://www.webinterpret.com
Take advantage of the International market and Increase your sales abroad by listing on multiple international eBay sites with the appropriate modifications and accurately translated by professional translators.

A picture can display the product you have for sale, but nothing compares to seeing it in action. These are the eBay approved video hosts who can display your products in action to your eBay buyers.

i2iAuction
http://www.i2iauction.com
Place an eBay streaming video with sound of your item into your eBay auction description.

AuctionMercial
http://www.auctionmercial.com/
Make video from photos and voice in seconds, sell with easily created video - Take your pictures, Add your voiceover.

vzaar
http://vzaar.com
Professional quality online video platform used by media companies, marketing agencies, corporate communications, e-commerce, web applications and non-profit organizations.

eCommercePlayer
http://www.ecommerceplayer.com/
Online audio and video hosting for e-commerce web sites, online auctions, family albums or even audio or video blogs.

AuctionVideo
http://www.auctionvideo.com/
Explain what the selling item is, why people will want it, demonstrate how it works, and show its authenticity with AuctionVIDEO.

CarThink
http://www.carthink.com/
CarTHINK Movie Gallery uses still photos - no shooting required for high-end production with low-end cost.

Google Videos
http://video.google.com/
Google video hosting.

Microsoft Bing Videos
http://www.bing.com/videos/browse
Microsoft Bing video hosting.

MySpace Videos
http://www.myspace.com/videos
MySpare video hosting.

Silverdock
http://silverdock.com/
Digital video agency focused exclusively on video for eCommerce including video production, consulting, and video deployment.

YouTube
http://www.youtube.com/
YouTube video hosting.

Daily Motion
http://www.dailymotion.com/us
Share your videos publicly, or privately with family and friends and spread your videos across the web by posting them to your blog, website, or social network profiles.

Collect+

20% off your first shipment. Simply enter the following promotion code *"tamebay"* on the payment screen at www.collectplus.co.uk. (only one promo code allowed per user)

Jane Bell
email: ebay@JaneBell.co.uk
Offer: Free 30 minute virtual consultation/store critique.

Frooition
http://www.frooition.com
Offer: 5% discount. Quote discount code *"TBD2011"*

Tradebox
http://www.tradebox.uk.com
Offer: 10% Discount off Tradebox. Quote Tamebay eBay Tools and Services Guide 2011.

myHermes
http://www.myhermes.co.uk
Offer: 10% first time use. Quote code *"TBHB001"*

As Was
http://www.aswas.com
One-time discount of 10% off their contract total. Just quote TAMEBAY

Advansys
http://www.advansys.com
Offer: 10% off eBay Store Designs. Quote Code: AdeBay2011

Dzine Hub
http://www.dzine-hub.com/
Offer: Get 5% OFF on your custom eBay store design & listing template design package with Dzine-Hub. Here at Dzine-Hub, we offer you the best designs, coupled with unmatched service levels to guide you through the simple procedure of getting your eBay store design and listing template design done. Quote Coupon Code: TAMEBAY5